CW01510495

The **TUDOR** Dynasty

Margaret Beaufort

of

Bourne,

Collyweston, Maxey and Deeping

Margaret Wainwright

Grosvenor House
Publishing Limited

This book is published by
Grosvenor House Publishing Ltd
Link House
140 The Broadway, Tolworth, Surrey, KT6 7HT.
www.grosvenorhousepublishing.co.uk

A CIP record for this book
is available from the British Library

ISBN 978-1-83975-368-8

**Dedicated to my grandchildren
Benjamin, Daniel, Eloise and Julia**

'To know the past is to know the future'
Julia Salmon (Age 9)

There is a difference between obsession and devotion.

Contents

v

Introduction

I couldn't believe it!

I have lived in Bourne all my life apart from five years away as student.

As a child, I lived in St. Peter's Road, Bourne, which sadly no longer looks as idyllic as it once did, with the marching on of industrial progress.

In my childhood, we children 'owned' the Well Head fields at the end of our road. This was our playground. We knew how to avoid wet patches in the marshy parts of the field; we knew how to avoid the cowpats (well most of them); we knew where the thistles were and we knew the best places to build a den.

The fields were largely left as nature dictated. The pool was no great place to catch sticklebacks with our trusty nets but the South Street stream was a rich source and, armed with our 2lb CWS (co-op) jam jars, we would take our catch and put them in the Well-Head pool in the hopes that it would become a more fertile source in the future.

In those days, a small bridge enabled us to traverse the horse pool, now filled in, and also the main pool with a rather picturesque stile at the end, that would lead to the main south field.

This was the scene for many adventures and it was very rare for any other soul to venture across the somewhat neglected terrain.

Hence my total surprise when recently reading Philippa Gregory's book, 'The Red Queen', that Margaret Beaufort, the main character and indeed the 'Red Queen' herself, not only lived for a while in Lincolnshire but actually in Bourne for five years. Not only this, but actually she took up residence in the castle on her own lands on the Well Head!

As a Bourne girl, or 'Brunnian' as we are known, I was very conversant with our great celebrities of the past. We boast of Hereward the Wake, Robert Manning, Lord Cecil Burghley, who was born here, Charles Worth, the fashion designer, Raymond Mays, of the racing cars fame but never of this famous woman who was the great matriarch of the Tudor dynasty! Had she lived at a time when a woman could inherit the Crown, she would have been the Queen of England and along with Elizabeth I, Victoria and Elizabeth II, she would have counted as one of the greatest.

This is the mother of Henry VII, the grandmother of Henry VIII, the great grandmother of Mary Tudor, Edward VI and Elizabeth I, none of whom would have inherited the Crown without her amazing tenacity during the Wars of the Roses, a time when she had to fight, not just for Henry's crown, but for their very survival.

Her royal blood is the only link between William the Conqueror and our present queen, even though the continuity is a little frail at times. The more research I completed on this woman, the more important I realised she was and how very significant she was in Bourne and its surrounding area.

The existence of a castle in Bourne (indeed her castle) has been widely disputed over the years but to me there seems to be no doubt whatsoever; there is far too much evidence, both in tracing its past owners and the physical evidence that can be seen today, to dispute this fact.

It would appear from historical accounts that the grounds of the castle were used in Saxon times and the names of the owners can be found but I have concentrated on the owners only from the Norman times.

So it is my intention to share with the people of Bourne, Maxey, Deeping and Collyweston in particular, the results of my research into this woman who has been so wrongly overlooked in our local history.

I am no historian and do not wish to give the impression that I am an authority here. I am writing this in the 2020 'Covid 19' lockdown and my ability to search through primary material is not possible (it is usually in Latin or French, so I am quite happy to have an excuse!) and I freely admit to having to rely on the secondary sources at my disposal. Kenneth Jacob has something to say on this point.

He states:

'It is principally from primary source material... that a history can be built up and not, on the whole, from secondary sources or tertiary sources'[1].

Do not consider my writings to be a great historical study, it isn't. I would just like to give Margaret Beaufort the recognition that she so richly deserves in our community and to share with you all my

---

[1] Kenneth Jacobs 'Bourne and its Castle' (2005)

findings and, hopefully, simplify the facts that I have found for easier reading.

In order to fully understand her significance, I feel it is necessary to include her lineage and some of the amazing characters that can be found in her ancestry along with evidence of our castle and its owners and also her presence in Maxey, Deeping and Collyweston.

Unfortunately (for me), I felt it necessary to include facts about the Wars of the Roses, which is a maze of intrigue and changing loyalties with many bloody consequences, in order to have a more comprehensive understanding of this woman and her significant place in English history.

1

Margaret Beaufort's Early Life

Margaret Beaufort was born on 31st March 1443 at Bletsoe Castle in Bedfordshire. This 'manor' belonged to her mother, Margaret Beauchamp, who owned several other properties. Her father was John Beaufort, Earl and later Duke of Somerset, a descendant of Edward III, who was her great grandfather.

Edward III had seventeen children, all of whom could rightly say they had a claim to the throne, which of course led towards the Wars of the Roses in years to come. Margaret's family were descendants of John of Gaunt, Duke of Lancaster, Edward III's fourth son who was one of the richest men in England.

John of Gaunt's first wife was Blanche, daughter and heir of Henry, Duke of Lancaster. Together they had seven children, three of whom survived beyond infancy. The most notable son became Henry IV who in 1399 allegedly starved his cousin, Richard II, to death (the son of Edward III's first son, 'The Black Prince') in order to secure the throne for himself.

However, John of Gaunt had a mistress called Katherine Swynford whilst he was still a married man. Together they had four children out of wedlock. When Blanche died (his first wife) John married Katherine in 1396 but this did not legitimise their children. In order to sufficiently provide for these children, he honoured them with the name 'Beaufort' after one his castles in Champagne.

However, when Richard II was on the throne, he legitimised these children, his cousins, but it was made clear that they would be barred from ever having any claim on the throne!

Here then was the origin of the House of Lancaster, one of the formidable families of the Wars of the Roses. John Beaufort I, Duke of Somerset, died in 1410 and was followed in turn by his son, also named John Beaufort, who died in 1444 and who was the father of Margaret Beaufort, placing her well and truly in the 'Lancastrian side'.

Sadly, Margaret's father had a 'wasted life'[1]   He was a military man and accompanied the Duke of Clarence to France in the 'Hundred Year War'. He was defeated in the Battle of Bange in 1421 and captured, along with his younger brother, Thomas.

This was the beginning of his social and political demise. The brothers were kept in captivity for about seven years in France before a ransom could be agreed for their release, which proved to be particularly costly. He returned home after an absence of seventeen years to a life that was basically alien to him. He failed as a landowner, some of these lands being in Deeping. According to the 'Crowland Chronicles'[2], he wanted to make his lands a success but with little to no experience, this was to prove an impossible task.

---

[1] Elizabeth Norton.
[2] The 'Crowland Chronicles' online Wikipedia (May 2020)

On his arrival home, at first, he had been greeted with much joy and enthusiasm from his tenants but this soon waned when he started to demand unrealistic taxes from them in order to find the funds to pay off his ransom money.

His unpopularity was further compounded when, in the reign of the new king, Henry VI, who was a mere infant at the time of Henty V's death, John Beaufort II was sent as a military commander to defend Gascony. The only reason he was appointed to this task was possibly his royal blood but it proved to be a dreadful disaster. He pillaged Brittany, an ally of England at the time, which provoked an uproar at home. He was summoned to return home. Reputedly, he cost the crown £26,000 and he was in disgrace for this error of judgement.

Eight months later when he returned to England, he was refused an audience with the king and was banished from court. This was an unexpected disgrace on his part and when he realised that he faced a charge of treason, he committed suicide in 1444.

What a start in life for poor Margaret! At one year old, she was left fatherless, a matter that was well documented in the Crowland Chronicles. However, as her father's only legitimate child, on his demise she became a very wealthy heiress. Although her estates were lost to her for a short time in the Wars of the Roses, basically, throughout her life, she enjoyed being one of the wealthiest women in England. Had her father not taken his own life, his estates may have returned to the Crown and Margaret would have been left in relative poverty.

Perhaps because of this early disaster in her life and the fact that she was a significant landowner, helped to make Margaret the gritty, political and shrewd woman that she undoubtedly became.

However, wealth for a woman at this time was also a liability. A woman, in this period of history, fared better if she had a protector.

Margaret's wealth would certainly have given her an eligible position on the marriage market.

Her wardship was granted, firstly to William De La Pole, 1st Duke of Suffolk, who was himself one of the wealthiest, most powerful men in England. His power cannot be underestimated as Henry VI was still so young. In fact, it was mainly due to him that Margaret d'Anjou was chosen to be Henry VI's wife.

Happily for Margaret, she was allowed to stay with her mother at this time. They spent much of their time at Bletsoe in Bedfordshire and in another of her mother's castles in Maxey. Her mother was an educated woman and ensured that Margaret received an education far superior to that which was expected for females at the time. She was educated to speak French fluently but regretted not learning Latin. However, in later life she rectified this deficiency and became a leading educationalist. Her mother was regarded as very pious and this trait became one of Margaret's notable features.

Margaret's early life was not to remain a peaceful time. At the early stages of the Wars of the Roses her protector, Suffolk had become a very unpopular man, especially with the common people and with the York side of the family. He was regarded as greedy acting largely out of self-interest. He was imprisoned in the Tower but still had his eyes on Margaret's wealth and property. No doubt he was aware that the Lancaster House did not have an heir, therefore Margaret's position was further enhanced as her marriage could well see her future husband on the throne of England. To this end, Margaret found herself married to his son, John De La Pole at the tender age of eight.

Suffolk's scheming plans, however, were eventually thwarted. He was accused of arranging an invasion of England to destroy Henry VI and of handing back France to Henry's uncle, Charles VII. Whether or not these charges were all justified, it resulted in him being exiled in 1450. Sadly for him, his ship was intercepted on its journey by a second ship, the 'Nicholas of the Tower', and he was given a mock trial by the sailors. He was found guilty of all charges and beheaded with a rusty sword, which took six strikes to finish the deed. He was buried later at 'Charterhouse' in Kingston upon Hull, where my own grandmother lived at the end of her life!

Margaret had lost the first of the several protectors in her life. Her wardship passed to the Crown but she was allowed to stay in the comfort of her mother's home. Soon however, her wardship was passed to the king's half-brothers, Edmund and Jasper Tudor, both of whom had been in the care of Suffolk's sister, Katherine de La Pole. This was perhaps the happiest possible outcome for Margaret as it would shape her whole future.

Edmund, the Earl of Richmond, and Jasper, the Earl of Pembroke, were the sons of Catherine de Valois, wife of Henry V and the mother of Henry VI. When Henry V died, Catherine secretly married Owen Tudor, a man considered to be well below her station. She had been in love with Margaret's uncle, Edmund Beaufort, but despite their love for each other Edmund felt that to marry her himself would be a very poor political move for her and he was not prepared to make her suffer. The fact that she married Owen quickly and in secret and that her first son was called Edmund … could possibly be a little scandal?!

With Suffolk's death and disgrace and despite being only twelve years of age, Margaret was allowed a choice. She could either remain married to John De La Pole, whom she had probably never even met, or she could marry Edmund Tudor.

Folk law or truth, she apparently had a dream that she should marry Edmund and what an inspired choice this was for her to make. Of course, at this point, she was not considered important as an heiress in the Lancastrian line because Henry VI and Margaret d'Anjou did produce a male heir, Edward of Lancaster. On 1st November 1455, Edmund Tudor married Margaret Beaufort.

She was not physically mature enough for the consummation of a marriage, but it seems that Edmund was not prepared to wait. Three months after the wedding, Margaret unknowingly was carrying the future King of England.

Her safety was considered paramount, as the Wars of the Roses were already in the early stages, so consequently Margaret was taken to Jasper's castle in Pembroke, a fair distance from any warlike action.

This was a fortuitous decision. Her husband, Edmund, died three months later whilst Margaret was still only six months pregnant. She remained in Pembroke but had once more lost her protector, though she was fortunate to have Jasper, her brother-in-law, close by to look after her. Indeed, he looked after her throughout her life and protected her 'soon-to-be-born' son, living long enough to see this son on the throne of England as Henry VII.

Childbirth was traumatic for Margaret; at the age of thirteen, she was too under-developed to go through the rigours of childbirth. Both mother and child were expected to die but somehow both survived. Sadly, the physical damage to Margaret meant that this would be her only child.

Now Margaret began to show her true grit in life. She was not going to have decisions made for her anymore. She knew that she would need another protector, even more so now that she had a politically important child to care for. She decided that she must marry again.

Within four months of Edmund's death, she chose a husband before anyone else could find one for her. Her choice was Henry Stafford, the husband to whom she was married during her time in

Bourne. She was betrothed to him before the accepted time for mourning had passed and married very quickly; this young girl, at the age of fourteen, was already on her third husband.

She had sound reasons for choosing Henry. He had royal connections being descended from Thomas Woodstock, the youngest son of Edward III. This connection meant that he could, in theory, have a claim to the throne.

His father, the Duke of Buckingham, was the only peer in England at the time with a lineage to rival Richard, Duke of York, who was descended from Edward III's second son, Lionel of Antwerp. His mother, Anne Neville (not the renowned Anne who married Richard III) was the daughter of Margaret Beaufort's great aunt, Joan Beaufort. Their family ties were so close that they had to obtain a dispensation from the Pope to allow them to marry.

Further self-will and determination were shown at her son's christening. Until that day he was to be called 'Owen' after his Tudor grandfather. However, it would seem that by the time they had left the church, she had decreed his name should be 'Henry' after her Lancastrian king and kinsman.

Although this marriage was initially of political convenience, it would appear that Margaret and Henry did have a happy marriage although no further children were added to her household. Stafford was thirty-one years old when he married Margaret, almost twenty years her senior. Sadly, he seemed to suffer from ill-health with a skin complaint known as, 'St Anthony's Fire' or 'Holy Fire', apparently a form of leprosy.

In fact, this may have proved a blessing in disguise! During the Wars of the Roses he proved he was not a man who found it politic to ally with either side, consequently he would be able to keep in the background on several occasions, pleading ill-health.

He was a kindly and amicable man but with little wealth of his own, being a second son. Thus, the marriage was very suitable for both of them. Margaret was blessed that, as the King had produced an heir, her son Henry was no longer as important as a candidate for the throne and she was able to have him with her for at least a while.

Margaret and Henry Stafford came to live in Bourne at this time, in 1458, in the castle and lands that she had inherited from her father. Bourne had been in possession of the Holland Family and they had entertained Edward III here for a week. The castle was set 'in beautiful parklands with fine rooftops overlooking the Fens'[3]. The house where Margaret and Henry lived was of 'Norman origin, a large motte-and-bailey castle that featured a keep and was entered through a medieval gatehouse that may have led to a courtyard, as well as to entertain visitors, most probably in the hall'[4].

Margaret was obviously very fond of Bourne as in her first will of 1472, she stated that she would like to be buried here. In fact, as she later became so significant as the mother of the King, she was buried in Westminster Abbey. However, Bourne was not forgotten by her and at the end of her life she made a bequest of a mass book to Bourne Abbey in her will. Despite efforts to rediscover this, its whereabouts remain a mystery, at present.

Margaret would have worshipped in Bourne Abbey Church where her great-grandfather, Thomas Holland, the Earl of Kent lay buried in the graveyard. The Abbey Church suffered during the Dissolution of the Monasteries in Henry VIII's time, but the main aisle and surrounding arches remain intact; it is a fully functioning church to this day with a splendid choir singing on Sunday morning services and choral evensong each month (author and husband are in the choir!).

---

[3] Elizabeth Norton 'Margaret Beaufort: Mother of the Tudor Dynasty' (2010)

[4] E. Venables 'Bourne and its Abbey and Castle' Associated Architectural Society, Rep arts and Paper 20

Margaret and Henry's disquiet can only be fully realised by looking at their position in the Wars of the Roses. They left Bourne about five years later and spent much of their time at their castle in Woking, Surrey, once in the possession of Edward the Confessor and like Bourne, it had passed into the hands of the Holland Family. On the marriage of Margaret Holland to John Beaufort I, Margaret's grandfather, it became part of the Beaufort estates.

Woking was a very large and luxurious property and the couple remained here managing their estate in the 1460s. They were able to enjoy hunting, a favourite pastime, on the Windsor estate. In 1467, she had another rare meeting with her son, Henry, who was still with his protector, Jasper Tudor, in Raglan Castle.

However, peace was not to be enjoyed by Margaret for long as her fortunes suddenly seemed to turn from one disaster to another, testing the great mettle of the woman. Just as the wars were becoming even fiercer, Henry Stafford died in 1482, probably from the injuries he sustained at the Battle of Tewkesbury, leaving Margaret in a very vulnerable and unprotected position once more. Not only this her king, Henry VI was imprisoned in the Tower, leaving the Lancastrian line to face a fearful position; she had to let her son flee to exile with her brother-in-law, Jasper. She must have felt completely deserted and fearful. Edward IV, who had deposed Henry VI, had shown himself to be ruthless to his enemies and towards any claimants to his throne; Margaret was clearly on 'the wrong side'. A slight comfort for her could have been in that Henry Stafford referred to her in his will as his 'entirely and best-beloved wife' and, despite her own wealth, he saw that she was well-provided for by leaving her all his possessions, apart from his horses.[5]

---

[5] N. Tallis (P112) TNA PROB (11 July 2012)

Margaret realised her position was precarious, leaving her with one real option. Being a wealthy woman gave her great status on the 'marriage market' and so she chose her fourth husband quickly and wisely. She could see the dangers of being allied solely to the Lancastrian line, and so chose a man with a firm place with the Yorkists, Thomas Stanley.

This choice was particularly shrewd. Not only did Thomas have a very influential Yorkist brother, William, but both brothers were masters at spreading their allegiance between both houses. Eventually, at the Battle of Bosworth, neither had committed to either side at first. Only during the battle itself did William choose the Lancastrian side, which determined the outcome in favour of Henry, Margaret's son, who was crowned on the battlefield as Henry VII.

The couple seemed to have a harmonious marriage despite Thomas having to keep Margaret under house arrest after she had been accused of treason during a failed attempt to secure Henry's ascent to the throne. Certainly, she would have been executed for her crimes against the King had Thomas and William not been of such value to King Richard III, the king at the time of her unsuccessful plot. Richard feared the Stanleys' abilities to gather troops against him and therefore agreed to a more lenient sentence.

The Battle of Bosworth was possibly the worst moment of Margaret's life, knowing that if the Lancastrians lost, not only would she lose her own life as a traitor but she would lose her precious son either in battle or on the scaffold. How must she have felt when the battle was won, and her son walked towards her with the crown on his head?

As the Mother of the King, we can see that she became the matriarch of the whole Tudor dynasty. However, she did not retire in any way following this victory; she became more and more influential in royal circles and in her educational influence. Much of her work can still be seen and experienced today, such is her lasting influence.

Through this part of her life, she spent much time in Collyweston, where she lived in luxury in a large castle when she was not at the Royal Court. She remained married to Thomas Stanley and their relationship seemed harmonious. However, she took an oath of chastity, which gave her independence from her husband, so giving her the freedom to be a very influential woman in her own right.

Sadly, she outlived her son who died in April 1509. Margaret died two months later in June 1509 but she lived long enough to see her second grandson, Henry VIII, safely on the throne of England.

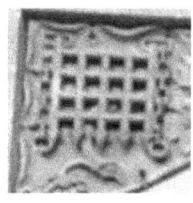

2

Margaret Beaufort – The person

Margaret's life was a roller coaster of wealth and poverty, stability and frantic disaster. So many of her family were either killed in battle, executed or, like her father, had committed suicide. Throughout all this, Margaret had to steer a course of diplomacy and humility in order to survive but at the same time had to keep her strong resolve and courage. What an achievement then in her finest hour, to see her son crowned on the battlefield by non-other than her husband Thomas Stanley.

Margaret's family always had to face the fact that their line was illegitimate. John of Gaunt produced his line of Beauforts whilst still married to his first wife, even though he did eventually marry his mistress, Katherine Swynford. Richard II, John of Gaunt's nephew, did legitimise them but with the proviso that no-one in their line of descendancy could ever have a claim to the throne. Margaret would know this and must have wondered when this question of Henry VII's legitimacy could rear up and deprive him of the throne she had fought so hard to gain for him.

The character of Margaret cannot be fully explained without an examination of her part in the Wars of the Roses. Like most key players in this troubled period of history, she had the wisdom to hide her true feelings and learned when to bide her time.

Philippa Gregory's portrayal of Margaret was perhaps inspired, in no small part by the dour and only painting of her in her lifetime, now hanging in St John's College, Cambridge.[6] In Phillipa Gregory's novel, the overwhelming feeling with which one is left, is that she was overzealous in her piety and in her ambition for her son Henry at the cost of all other people and interests. This is partly true but there are far more sides to this woman.

The only physical descriptions of her suggest she had 'hooded eyes; was of slender frame; had a narrow face, much like Henry VII and was 'Never a tall woman' but was sometimes described as beautiful and had 'keen searching eyes'[7].

There is no doubt that she was pious, as her mother was before her, and she was obviously disciplined in her duty to prayer. Looking at her life, at times this must have been her one consolation and comfort.

Her days at Collyweston bore witness to this pious dedication in particular. Henry Parker, Lord Morley, who worked for her for over forty years said ,'her grace was every morning in the chapel betwixt five and seven of the clock, and dayly sayde matins of the day with one of her chaplyns, and that sayde from sevyn tyll yt was eleven off the clocks, as sone as one priest had sayd masses in her sight another beganne, one tyme in a day she was confessyd, then going to her dynner how honourably she was servydI think few Kings better.[8]

---

[6] 'The Red Queen' by Philippa Gregory (2010)
[7] Elizabeth Tallis
[8] Chambers Cyclopedia of English Literature Tallis

Under her clothing, she wore shirts and girdles of hair to enhance her religious dedication, which apparently made her skin very sore. According to Elizabeth Norton, 'Even in her old age, Margaret was renowned for fasting especially in Lent when she 'restrayned her appetite one mele and tylone fyshe on the day.''[9]   Sadly, she even prayed so hard that she injured her knees and back, particularly when she was in Woking where she could 'focus on her piety.' The favoured Saints to whom she prayed were Mary Magdalene, St Catherine, and St Anthony, the latter possibly because she could appeal to him to help with her third husband's skin complaints.

In her later life, John Fisher became a great friend to Margaret. He was a very clever and well-educated man firstly, an English Catholic Bishop, then Cardinal and eventually served as Chancellor of Cambridge University. He spoke at her funeral and went into great detail about her piety 'for which she was famous', going on to say she was 'to God and to the churche full obedient and tractable'.[10]

However, there was far more to Margaret's character which seems to have been overlooked in the traditional presentation of her life.

Margaret was certainly a very strong-willed woman, a trait which seemed to first show itself at the christening of her son. On arrival for the service, it seems to have been established that her son would be called 'Owen' after his Welsh Tudor grandfather. Margaret changed this, and he was christened Henry after her deceased husband's half-brother, the King. She continued in this vein throughout her life, finally gaining complete independence during her last marriage, taking an oath of chastity and being granted the position of 'Femme Sole'. This put her status above

---

[9] Elizabeth Norton ' Margaret Beaufort: Mother of the Tudor Dynasty' (2010)
[10] Elizabeth Norton from 'Early English Books online' quoting John Fisher 'Mornynge Remembrance' (2010)

that of her husband and she was able to manage her own lands and estates. This was almost un-heard of for a woman of this era.

On a far lighter side, she apparently enjoyed gambling, playing cards, hunting, festive music and reading. After lunch each day, she was entertained by jesters, where there was much laughter at her table 'of the begynnyng of her dyner was to be joyous and heare those tales that were honest to make her mery.'[11]

At Christmas, she would entertain on a lavish scale and Morris Dancers were part of the entertainment. She invited many nobles along but she ensured that her servants were also well fed and included in the festivities. Indeed, at New Year she gave her gentlewomen jewels that she had purchased in London. All was royally decorated, enhanced by her beautiful tablecloth, 'with Tudor roses and Margaret's own Beaufort portcullis badge'.[12] She had cushions of silk, velvet and cloth of gold.

She very much enjoyed fine clothes and jewellery. Indeed, at her castle in Collyweston, she had a room put aside for her jewellery and sometimes 'employed the service of a Stamford goldsmith'. Amongst her possessions was a fine pomander decorated with marguerite daisies, 'daisy' being a derivative of the name Margaret. When Henry became king, Margaret often wore a rich coronall (coronet) 'Such was the demeanour of the woman who behaved as though she was a queen'.[13]

She was equally interested in clothes. At the coronation of Elizabeth of York, she wore the same outfit as her daughter-in-law to emphasise her own royal status. At Henry's coronation, she

---

[11] E. Norton
[12] E. Norton
[13] E. Norton (pp*)

appeared 'Magnificently dressed, and she received ten yards of scarlet cloth from the king'.[14]

Even when married to Henry Stafford, they enjoyed many luxury items. 'She and Stafford always liked to appear well dressed'.[15] She had a great 'interest in rich fabrics' and 'Her receiver recorded that sums were paid for furring a gown for her, an expensive process'.[16] She loved velvet and often sent to London for the latest fashions, all showing her wealth and status, a far cry from the dour painting that hangs in St John's Cambridge. John Fisher himself remarked that 'she lived in luxury and was able to entertain on a lavish scale'. On her death, her jewels and plate were worth £2,805,000 in today's money. Altogether, including her lands and estates, she was worth £100,000,000.

Not only did she own the castle and lands in Bourne, Collyweston and Maxey, she was in possession of other properties, many having been given to her by her son Henry VII once he was on the throne. She owned Woking, which was so luxurious that Henry took it from her, but it was reinstated on his death. In 1487, she acquired Corfe Castle, previously owned by her father. She acquired the House of Sheen in 1501 and although this burnt down, it was rebuilt and renamed 'Richmond'. She was given property in Devon, Hertfordshire, Westmorland and Tattershall Castle, in Lincolnshire.

Her wealth cannot be questioned but for such a powerful, strong willed woman, it might be expected that she would be somewhat selfish and indulgent, but this was not the case.

Whilst at Collyweston, she had four hundred and forty servants but always amazed everyone as she knew all their names. She

---

[14] E. Norton

[15] E. Norton

[16] E. Norton (*)

took a personal interest in them and if any should fall ill, she would visit them and help them.

Fisher described how she maintained twelve poor people and gave them, 'lodgings, food and clothing'.[17] He said she supported priests and even visited one in prison. Fisher stated, 'She was Mercyfull also...and to them that were in poverty or sekeness or any other mysery.' She is remembered as the foundress of an alms house built for women near the Chapel of St Anne, Westminster. He continued to say she was 'Bounteous and liberal to every person of her knowledge and acquaintance.'[18] On a visit to Boston, Lincolnshire, it was reported that she gave a child a coin for singing to her.

She gave out the Maundy money just before Easter, and Vergil is quoted as saying, 'she was a most worthy woman (whom) no one can extol too much or too often for her sense of holiness of life'.[19]

Fisher went on to say she was of, 'mervayllous gentleness ...unto all folks' and that 'She was not vengeable ne cruel' and she would, 'forgive injuryes done.'[20]

Margaret must have been good company as her third and fourth marriages, despite being chosen for political reasons, seemed to be happy and harmonious. She and Stafford appeared to travel considerably and always together. She was married to him for thirty years and he described her as his loving wife. In his will, he left all his possessions to 'My beloved wife', apart from his horses which went to his brother.

However, a huge part of her life was dedicated to education. She was a well-educated woman which was unusual for her era. She

---

17 E. Norton quoting John Fisher
18 E. Norton quoting John Fisher
19 N. Tallis quoting 'Vergil Polydore Angelica Historia' (*)
20 E. Norton quoting John Fisher

would translate books from the Latin into English and became a very good patron of William Caxton, who could print her works quickly and afford her a greater audience. He was delighted to be recognised in court circles and so it was a mutually beneficial arrangement. He dedicated two books to her saying she was the 'Ladder to Perfection' and 'Of Excellent Bounty'

With the collaboration of John Fisher, she was able to establish centres of learning which continue to thrive today. John was born in 1484 in Beverley, Yorkshire and was regarded as being exceptionally educated. He was an English Catholic Bishop, Cardinal and theologian and became Bishop of Rochester and Chancellor of Cambridge University. He was a man of great integrity but his refusal to accept Henry VIII as Head of the Church, led to his death on the block in the Tower of London in 1535. However, Margaret had the highest regard for him for his learning and piety. He first came to her attention because of his great influence in educational circles and she was so impressed that she asked him to become a part of her household.

Margaret was interested in both Oxford and Cambridge universities but although she still took an interest in Oxford, she directed her interest largely to Cambridge. This centre of learning was closer to both Bourne and Collyweston and would have made her travels far easier. She was by no means a patron who simply donated money; she made frequent journeys to watch the progress of the colleges.

She began her patronage at Queen's College and Jesus College but then turned her attention to Christ's College in Cambridge. It is very easy to see her influence here today as her symbols and statues still embellish the buildings. At the doorways are the portcullis symbols which display the crown above them. The crowns were obviously a proud addition to reflect the royalty of the Tudors and Beauforts. Margaret commissioned the Beaufort Cup for the College, decorated with the portcullis, fleurs de lys, marguerites and roses.

She seems to have influenced her son, Henry VII, in taking an active interest in education, as a chest can still be seen today in the chapel, which he donated and was filled with money at the time.

St John's College benefited from her patronage; after a legal strife, she was able to convert a hospital into the college. She died before its completion, but Fisher completed her work after her death. It is at Christ's College, Cambridge where a recently, beautifully renovated statue of her can be seen.

Another of her achievements educationally, was to establish a grammar school in Wimborne Dorset, possibly because her parents were buried here. She obviously felt this would be a great tribute to their memory.

In conclusion, she seems to be a far cry from her portrayal in fiction, as an obsessive and insular character.

From her amazing input into the foundations of education in England alone, it still seems strange that this amazing woman has been so overlooked in the local history of Bourne, Collyweston, Maxey and Deeping. However, is there another reason why we ignore her? Not just perhaps, because she was a woman but could she possibly be guilty of the murder of the Princes in the Tower as has been suggested?

It is a pertinent question knowing how desperate she may have been to see her son, Henry, on the throne, an honour that would grant her the peace and security that had eluded her for most of her life.

3

Did Margaret Kill the Princes in the Tower?

In his work, 'Winter King: The Dawn of Tudor England,' Thomas Penn commented:

'Henry Tudor an avenging king come to claim his throne from Richard III, who had murdered his nephews and wrenched the true line of Yorkist dynasty off course.'[21]

Here is the great question - did the Lancastrians plot for Henry VII to ascend to the throne, demand the deaths of the two young princes, or was it Richard III, who was so insecure on his throne that he would not want the boys to remain alive in case arms were taken up against him in their name?

Looking at Margaret's life and character, it is difficult to believe that she would enter into such a murderous plot in order to get

---

[21] Thomas Penn 'Winter King: The Dawn of Tudor England' (Sept. 2011)

Henry on the throne. Richard III was the crowned king from 1483 and also had a son and heir Edward the Prince of Wales. Despite all of Margaret's ambitions, the throne for Henry must have seemed a distant fancy. Her son had been out of the country for many years and was virtually an unknown candidate.

Also, Margaret was so very close to John Fisher that he must have heard her confession many times. Would such a great and godly man feel comfortable in sharing such a dark sin?

Could it be that Richard III had more reason and opportunity to commit this dreadful crime? A closer look at Richard seems to be appropriate.

Certainly, Shakespeare portrayed him as a wicked hunchback and the murderer of the boys but he was writing for an Elizabethan audience and for Elizabeth herself.[22] The Court would have enjoyed this interpretation of the events. We do know, from the recent excavations in Leicester, that Richard certainly had a curvature of the spine but not to the degree portrayed in Shakespeare's play. Indeed, when he was faithfully fighting on the side of his brother, Edward IV, it is suggested that he was a fearsome and brave warrior, unhindered by his physical difficulties.

Richard was trusted by Edward IV both in battle and in politics, unlike their brother George, Duke of Clarence, who would change sides to support Warwick 'the King Maker' when it suited him. George, Duke of Clarence, was executed eventually in a barrel of malmsey for his treason.

Edward trusted Richard enough to declare on his death bed, that he would appoint Richard as regent to his sons, the future Edward V and his brother Richard, Duke of York.

---

[22] W. Shakespeare 'Richard III' (1593)

This does not portray Richard as a man who was dishonourable in any way or who could possibly imprison his nephews in the Tower only to murder them later. Would he be that callous? Could he be so villainous as to disregard his brother's wishes? Could two royal brothers, who had been so close, separate from their allegiances so dramatically? Well … maybe.

Once Edward IV had died, Richard acted quickly to bring the two boys under his control, away from their mother, Elizabeth Woodville, now the Dowager Queen. She feared for her own and their safety and sought the sanctuary of Westminster Abbey, taking her daughters and her son, young Richard, with her. It would seem that she felt she had reason to distrust Richard III and it seems she wanted any power he had over her boys to be removed.

For the boys' safety, Elizabeth wanted Edward crowned as soon as possible, so much so that she did not inform Richard (III) of his brother's death. Understandably, as the appointed protector of the boys, this would not have pleased him greatly.

Elizabeth sent her son, Edward (V) to London with her trusted brother, Anthony, Earl Rivers and her son by her first marriage, Sir Richard Grey, to act as his escorts. On the way, they stopped for the night at an inn. All seemed well but, unknown to them, it would seem that Richard (III) had acted quickly on the news of his brother's death and had ridden to Northampton, meeting up with the Duke of Buckingham with the intention to thwart Elizabeth's plan.

Neither held her in any regard, feeling that she was of low birth and, therefore, should not have any control over a future King of England. It was a popular perception of the time that she had tricked Edward IV into marriage, allegedly through witchcraft. Buckingham, the one-time father-in-law of Margaret Beaufort, resented her because she had been instrumental in securing his arranged marriage to her sister, whom he considered to be of, 'humble origins' and he disliked her intensely.

These two men, both with reason to dislike the Woodvilles, locked Rivers and Grey in their room, later taking them to Pontefract and executing them. Edward (V) was taken to the Tower 'for safe-keeping'.

At the time, this news was met with horror and apparently, even at this early stage, Richard's motives were greatly feared. It was suspected that he had brought the prince not into his care but into his power with the intention of claiming the Crown for himself.

Margaret would have been deeply disturbed by these events as they unfolded. The death of Edward IV would have been a bitter blow, not because she was a happy convert to the Yorkists but she was on the verge of negotiations with the King to reclaim lands that she had lost. She was on the verge of success when disaster struck. She did not have the confidence that her negotiations would be secure with Richard (III) in his new and powerful position.

By May 1483, many people suspected that Richard might be plotting to claim the throne as his own. Realising this, Richard set about removing his main opposition; many were nobles who had been staunch supporters of Edward IV and who were likely to support his sons.

On 17th June, in what today we might call 'false news', Richard (III) arrived at the Tower claiming that he had been ambushed by Hastings and the other right-hand men of Edward IV, including John Morton who were subsequently captured. They were taken to the Tower and Hastings was 'hacked to death'[23]. There was no trial for this man, who had done so much for his King and the country.

---

[23] N. Tallis

Even if there had been an ambush, Richard's retaliation seemed particularly brutal and unjust which was quite unlike the character that he seemed to be when his brother, Edward IV was king. One has to wonder why this change had arisen. Certainly, Richard's claim to the throne would be tenuous and he did appear to be removing all the possible stumbling blocks.

It was a turn of events that Hastings had not suspected. He had been warned that there was a plot being hatched against him the night before, but he dismissed this as being unlikely saying, 'be merry, have no fear'.[24]

Margaret must have been frantic at this turn of events as her husband Thomas Stanley was among those captured and imprisoned. Any taint of being labelled a traitor could affect them both but somehow Stanley was released. Richard may have feared the power of Lord Strange, Stanley's son by his first marriage, who would have been in a position to raise considerable troops against him.

Richard, at this point, had Edward (V) in his power but if anything happened to this boy, his brother would be able to inherit the Crown. Consequently, Richard now demanded that the younger boy should leave the sanctuary of Westminster Abbey and join his brother under his 'protection'. The fact that he said he would use force in order to procure him suggests this act favoured Richard III's interests rather than the young prince's protection.

Elizabeth obviously would not wish to compromise her own safety and that of her daughters. She allegedly allowed Richard, Duke of York, to be taken away to join his brother in the Tower. Whether this was Richard, or a substitute, was brought into question later.

---

[24] N. Tallis

Two usurpers, Perkin Warbeck and Lambert Simnel, both claimed to be him ... another mystery as yet unsolved.

Now Richard had the two boys under his control and their lives should have been protected carefully; on many occasions they were seen playing in the Tower gardens but after the summer they were never seen again. Edward was apparently quite unwell with respiratory problems and their doctor, Dr Argentine, did continue to visit for some time after the last sighting of the boys but was eventually barred from seeing them.

Comments at the time suggested that Richard (III) was becoming fairly open in his intentions but the date was set for Edward's coronation on 22nd June 1483. This came and went with no apparent preparations for this to happen. Then Buckingham, a supporter of Richard, along with other nobles, declared on 25th June that both boys were illegitimate because their father had already had a secret marriage to Eleanor Talbot before his agreed marriage to Elizabeth Woodville. This piece of information arrived in timely manner because on 26th June 1483 Richard was declared King of England.

Looking at Margaret Beaufort's position at this point, there would be little chance to ever hope that Henry could be king; Richard was now crowned, he had a son, Edward of Middleham. Cetainly there would be no challenge from the two princes now that they had been declared illegitimate by Parliament. Her concerns would have been focussed on how to survive this turn of events, now that the Yorkist family was in command and any opposition seemed to have been targeted and destroyed.

Richard III, on the other hand, could always fear an uprising against him. The Princes could always be used as a rallying point by people who wished to remove him.

On 6th July, Richard III and his wife, Anne Neville, were crowned in a lavish ceremony. Margaret Beaufort showed her aptitude for self-preservation over any loyalty to the Lancastrian House. She and Stafford both attended this coronation and wore clothing to match the event. However, Margaret's safety was not assured. Richard trusted neither Stafford nor his wife and, as Margaret was a wealthy landowner, this would have made her a lucrative target.

Margaret, in fact, was suspected of being involved in a plot to free the Princes in the Tower; the plot failed but Richard moved the boys into a more secure room within the centre of the building. One version of events suggested that Richard sent John Green to the Constable of the Tower, Sir Robert Brackenbury, demanding that he should put the two boys to death. Sir Robert refused to comply with this request prompting Richard to send Tyrell to demand the keys of the Tower from the Constable. The keys were relinquished to Sir James for the night, and Thomas Moore relates that the boys were smothered in their bedding and died.[25] Tyrell, at the end of his life, confessed to their murder in 1502.

Richard III wasted no time in declaring his son as the 'Prince of Wales'. No one at the time suggested that Margaret Beaufort or Henry Stafford (who was not in the country) were suspected of their murder.

Interestingly, Buckingham who had been so close to Richard, left his service at this point and joined forces with the Lancastrian side. Did he feel that Richard had gone too far? Admittedly, he did not stay loyal to anyone for long.

We now know today that the bodies of two young people have been found at the bottom of a staircase in the Tower of London and the material of their clothing would be such as befitting royal status. However, despite their bones being found and interred

---

[25] N. Tallis 'Commynes'

subsequently at Windsor Castle, no permission has been granted to exhume them for positive DNA testing.

I believe that we can exclude Margaret from any guilt of the murder of the princes, despite modern fiction pointing the finger of blame towards her. This was an age when thrones could be won and lost in short spaces of time and kings could be overthrown and killed. Richard seems to have exhibited his desire to remove any opposition through executions. Indeed, in looking at the progress of the Wars of the Roses, it is possible to see how Richard even set a trap for Henry (VII) tempting him to return to England. Without Margaret's watchful eye, Henry could well have fallen into it.

BUT...

Philippa Langley, who discovered Richard III's body in the Leicester car park and the members of the Richard III Society, would no doubt disagree.

Matthew Lewis, writer and historian has stated 'None of those closest to the princes accused Richard of murder - not even Elizabeth Woodville, the boys' mother'.[26]

Thomas Moore's take on Tyrell's confession was that there was no proof that he had killed them.

Matthew Lewis suggests that the Princes could have lived longer and into Henry VII's reign which would mean that Henry could have ordered their execution. However, Henry consulted Margaret on all his political choices and, knowing her character as illustrated earlier, it is not something that she would perhaps sanction; it would have been too much for her immortal soul.

---

[26] Matthew Lewis The Wars of the Roses (Aug. 2016)

It has been suggested that Buckingham was guilty of their murders as he had a firm claim to the throne through his Howard family lineage.

However, all these mysteries may never be solved and it is prudent to keep an open mind. New evidence does come to light and indeed a document that was destroyed in England, the 'Titulus Regius,' may have copies on the continent which could still reveal secrets. This was the only statute to be issued during Richard III's reign in 1484, declaring Richard's right to the throne.

For me, it is comforting, to believe that Margaret Beaufort seems to be innocent of the crime.

4

The Wars of the Roses

Like the Capulets and Montagues in 'Romeo and Juliet',[27] there was an 'ancient grudge' that arose between the descendants of Edward III to form for the most part, two warring factions - that of the House of Lancaster and the House of York.

Our 'Fair Maid of Kent' was the mother of Richard II. Richard II's father was the *first* son of Edward III, Edward the Black Prince. He was usurped by Henry IV, the son of John of Gaunt, Edward III's *third* son, with his first wife, Blanche. (Lancaster)

The York Family were descendants of Lionel of Antwerp through his daughter, Philippa, who married Edmund Mortimer. Their granddaughter, Ann Mortimer, married Richard, Earl of Cambridge and their union produced Richard, Duke of York!

Already confused?

---

[27] W. Shakespeare 'Romeo and Juliet' (1595-7)

Richard II was the King at the onset of all the troubles but in 1455, many barons resented the way in which Henry IV had taken his throne and no doubt were horrified by the way that Richard was treated in captivity. Their grievance was that Henry (IV) had no right to the throne and this continued to be their opinion in regard to Henry V and Henry VI.

Henry V had initiated the 'Hundred Years War', defeating France at the Battle of Agincourt, but Henry VI proceeded to lose all that his father had gained, leaving England with only Calais in its possession. More significantly, the wars drained the Treasury, leading to heavier taxes which, as it does today, caused much resentment. In addition, Henry VI, when he came to the throne, was often mentally unstable, a condition that he had inherited from his grandmother, Isabu of Bavaria.

To compound Henry's fragile position, he had two very unpopular advisers, Somerset (Edmund Beaufort, Margaret's uncle and possible father of Edmund Tudor) and Suffolk both of whom were apparently corrupt at court. (Henry VI's ambitious French wife, Margaret d'Anjou, was also unpopular).

Suffolk was unpopular for being responsible for the English defeat in France and also because he had sanctioned the marriage of Henry VI to Margaret d'Anjou, 'a dowerless princess'.[28]

By now the common people wanted blood and they looked to Richard of York to bring about change.

When Henry was 'mentally indisposed', Richard of York had been appointed as Lord Protector from 27th March 1454. He was a direct descendant of Edward III who possibly had as much right to the throne as Henry VI, especially as his predecessor was the

---

[28] Wikipedia (May 2020)

second son of Edward III, not the third son, who was John of Gaunt. Of the two, Richard, the greater statesman and warrior, would seem to be the better choice for King. Certainly, he seemed to think so and would want the Crown for his own head.

With much support from Parliament, Richard of York managed to impeach Suffolk.

Margaret Beaufort at the age of seven now entered politics, albeit unwittingly. Suffolk wanted the security of the large inheritance that was in Margaret's possession and as a consequence, drew up a marriage agreement between her and his son, John de la Pole. Suffolk, William de la Pole, was branded as a traitor and imprisoned in the Tower. As previously mentioned, from there he was condemned to be exiled in France for five years. However, vengeance was following him in the form of a ship, named 'Nicholas of the Tower' and he met his sudden and violent death at the hands of the sailors.

Margaret remained married to his son, John at this point, although she had probably never met him and the marriage was certainly not consummated.

Henry VI faced another assault on his authority when a man called, Jack Cade led a rebellion against the government on a march to London, between the months of April to July. Although the revolt was supressed, it 'contributed to the breakdown of royal authority that led to the Wars of the Roses.[29]

Now that Suffolk was removed from the scene, Margaret's uncle, Somerset, saw the opportunity to take a more powerful role in the government but above all men, Richard of York hated this one.

---

[29] N. Tallis 'Commynes Chronicler'

The Wars of the Roses begins...

These wars are far more complicated than I had first envisaged. Not only are there the two main families at war, but the personnel of those families changed allegiance when a political move was required. Then a third faction developed when Warwick became infuriated with Edward IV.

In my opinion, I cannot give a full account of Margaret's life without an explanation of her position in the wars, especially in her fight for Henry to inherit the throne.

I became confused at times in my research as to who was doing what, when, why, and to whom, and decided to present my findings as a timeline.

I am using symbols to show who began each new act of aggression, who won and who lost each 'round'. I have tried to keep to the main facts, but a wider reading of the events will prove to be very informative for interested readers.

Symbols

✂ The perpetrator of a battle

☺ The victor of the battle

☞ The Lancastrian moved to the Yorkist family

🖝 The Yorkist moved to the Lancastrian family

👎 Very bad times for Margaret Beaufort

👍 Better times for Margaret Beaufort

In the case of a future king, I have included their future title in brackets, e.g. Richard (III), Henry (VII).

The Wars of the Roses Part 1 Sequence of Events	
House of Lancaster	**House of York**
Henry VI is ill and incompetent.	
	Richard of York is appointed 'Protector', openly criticising Henry VI.
Henry VI recovers and assumes his role as King once more. Edward, his son, is born thus pushing York further down the accession position. Margaret d'Anjou and Somerset hate the possible threat of York to the throne.	
	Richard of York and Warwick, expecting an attack, establish an army.
Henry VI calls a King's Council of nobles but does not include Richard of York.	
	Richard of York's hatred of Somerset intensifies and he moves south to gather forces to destroy Somerset once and for all.
On 1st May 1454, Henry and Jasper travel to Leicester then onward to London, convinced that York was forming an army to take the throne. Somerset was more interested in fighting York to protect himself.	

1 ***22ⁿᵈ May 1454 - Battle of St Albans***	

	York tried to negotiate peace with the King; his terms were that he should surrender Somerset into his power.
Henry refused to pass Somerset over.	
	Even though he knew he would be guilty of treason, York attacked. Warwick led the attack, using the back lanes and guerrilla tactics securing victory. ✂☺
Humphrey, Duke of Buckingham, was badly prepared; he was captured and executed. Henry VI was injured by an arrow in his neck. Jasper was also injured and many of the dead were buried in St Alban's Abbey. Margaret Beaufort had now lost this powerful protector leaving her very vulnerable. ☞	

	Along with his victory, Richard of York had succeeded in gaining his revenge on Somerset for him sending him to Ireland as Governor in 1452, so excluding him from the Royal Court and Parliamentary influence. Consequently, Richard now satisfied, asked for the King's pardon for the past events.

Henry granted a pardon to Richard of York, and **peace** returned.

Henry seemed to want peace at first and he ordered his nobles to Westminster to settle a reconciliation. Had this been successful it would have been named, 'Loveday'. The King and Queen went 'hand in hand' to York to ensure that the line of succession would go to their son, Edward. However, Henry was still continuing to recruit an army.	

2
23rd September 1459 Battle of Blore Heath

On the Queen's orders, Lord Audley ambushed some of York's men in Staffordshire.	York's men were on their way to Ludlow to join their main army. (A good account of the battle can be found in Wikipedia).

3 12th October 1459 Battle of Ludford Bridge	
The Queen was mistrustful that York would honour her son's accession to the throne so attacked once more. ☺✂	
	Morale was low and men began to desert York's troops. York fled to Ireland and Warwick fled to Calais. The next day, the troops knelt before Henry VI and asked for pardon. In the November, York had all of his titles taken from him by an 'Act of Attainer'. Together, Edward (IV), son of Richard of York, along with Richard Neville (Warwick) raised an army in Sandwich to march on London.
Margaret d'Anjou took charge to consolidate her power over the government. They declared that York and his followers were guilty of high treason. Owen and Jasper Tudor reaped the benefit of this as they were awarded York's lands. Margaret Beaufort's father-in-law, Lord Welles was granted lands in Salisbury.	

	York began to gather troops in Ireland.
	On 26th June 1460, Warwick, Salisbury and Edward (IV), returned to England and went to London where they were welcomed with enthusiasm by the citizens.
In response, Henry VI, Margaret d'Anjou and Edward marched to Coventry and onwards to Northampton with 20,000 men.	
	Warwick and Salisbury marched to Northampton with 40,000 men, officially to simply plead their grievances to Henry VI.
Henry and Buckingham refused to hear them.	

4
10th July 1460 Battle of Northampton

	Warwick led his army against the King. ✂☺
Buckingham, Earl of Shrewsbury was killed. Henry VI was captured by an archer, Henry Mountfort, and led bareheaded to London. Margaret d'Anjou and Edward escaped to Harlech Castle. Margaret Beaufort and	

Stafford remained in the Lancastrian 'camp'. Stafford became the temporary head of the Buckingham family, but the title soon went to his 5-year-old nephew, Henry Stafford.	

8th September 1460

Margaret d'Anjou fled to Scotland.	
	York returned from Ireland and gained support in Wales. He marched to London, this time to claim the throne. He arrived on 10th October and claimed the throne on 16th October. Parliament decreed that Henry VI should still be King but Edward, his son, would no longer be in the line of succession. York was once more pronounced 'Protector' of England and his line would inherit the Crown.
Margaret d'Anjou was furious that her son was disinherited and proceeded south with Percy, Clifford and Somerset. All these men had lost their fathers at St Albans and had reason to hold a grievance against the Yorkists.	
	York and Salisbury marched north to meet them.

5
31st December 1460 Battle of Wakefield

Margaret d' Anjou had raised a greater force than York, commanded by the Duke of Somerset. <div align="center">☺✂</div>	
	York's army were undisciplined and were too busy pillaging. York and his eldest son were slain, Salisbury was captured and slain and their heads were exhibited on spikes above Mickelgate Bar in York. York's surviving son (Edward IV), became Earl of March and was determined to wreak revenge.
Jasper Tudor was now determined to quash this latest threat and marched his army to Herefordshire.	

6
2nd February 1461 Battle of Mortimer Cross

Owen and Jasper Tudor led their army into battle. Jasper fled the battle scene, but Owen was captured and executed in the marketplace in Hereford. It was considered a very savage battle.	Edward (IV) led his army into battle, but their losses were heavy. <div align="center">☺</div>

7 ***17th February 1461 2nd Battle of St Albans***	
Henry and Margaret d'Anjou were reunited but were increasingly unpopular and had to retreat.	
	Warwick now had the upper hand and wanted to stop the Lancastrian forces from reaching London. Edward (IV) reached London to be greeted with joyous enthusiasm. Henry VI was captured. ✂ ☺
Decree at Baynard's Castle	
Henry was released but on joining Margaret d'Anjou, they were at liberty to challenge Edward once more. Henry, with Somerset and Welles, went to York for the next challenge. For once, Stafford, Margaret Beaufort's husband, also had to go. Up until now they had remained in **Bourne** enjoying a relatively peaceful existence.	
	Edward IV's popularity continued to gather support for his position.

After 17th February 1461	
The Lancastrians failed to take action to secure the throne. Henry asked for a truce.	Edward (IV) saw the need to secure his claim to the throne as quickly as he could and began recruiting men.

February 1461	
	Edward joined Warwick and together they marched to London to wage war.

8
29th March 1461 Battle of Towton

This battle was named, 'Bloody Meadow' and the blood of hundreds of men mixed with the snow. The 'Croyland Chronicler' (Crowland) stated 28,000 men died. 'The blood of the slain, mingling with the snow, which at this time covered the whole surface of the earth, afterwards ran down in furrows and ditches along with the melted snow, in a most shocking manner for a distance of 2 or 3 miles.'[30]

	The verdict was that so many men had lost their lives that it was not regarded as a great victory. ✂☺
28th June 1461, Henry VI, Margaret d'Anjou and their son, Edward fled to Scotland. Margaret Beaufort's cousin,	
Henry Beaufort, also fled and was now branded as a traitor. ☜	

---

[30] N. Tallis quoting 'Crowland Chronicles'

Henry Stafford	Warwick presented as the real power behind the throne. Richard (III), Edward (IV)'s brother was created, the 'Duke of Gloucester'. Henry Stafford was pardoned and swore allegiance to Edward (IV) and the Yorkists in 1462. Warwick was created High Admiral and Steward of the Duchy of Lancashire. Edward was now the 'master and Governor of the whole realm' (Milanese Observer). He was very popular and was a brave and handsome warrior. He was known as a merciful and natural leader.
	Now that Stafford had joined Edward IV, Margaret Beaufort's lands were safe once more and she had less to worry about as regards Henry(VII)'s safety.
	Strangely, at this point, Edward chose to deprive Jasper of his castle in Pembroke. This inevitably would incur his anger. William Herbert, Henry (VII)'s guardian, was granted this property thus ensuring that all of Wales was in Edward's possession.

Henry (VII) was placed under Herbert's wardship at Raglan Castle. Margaret Beaufort had no option but to accept this decision. Luckily, Herbert had a great liking for Henry and treated him as one of his own family, giving him an education appropriate to his rank.	
	All Henry's lands and titles were claimed by Edward IV and given to his brother George, 'Duke of Clarence'.
Margaret Beaufort still referred to Henry (VII) as the 'Lord of Richmond'. Naturally, Jasper was furious at the turn of events depriving him of Pembroke and went north to Scotland to join forces with Henry VI whilst Margaret d'Anjou went to France to seek help from Louis XI.	
Edmund Beaufort ☞ ☞ ☞ ☞ ☞ ☞	Somerset, Edmund Beaufort, now tired of exile, joined Edward IV and became his 'Captain of the Guard' receiving a general pardon on March 10th.
	Edward also pardoned other members of Margaret Beaufort's family.

Somerset left Edward IV and joined Margaret d'Anjou in France. She forgave him and was delighted to get his support.	
	Somerset Edmund Beaufort
	Edward was outraged by this defection and imprisoned Somerset's mother in retaliation. He became very antagonistic towards the Beaufort family.

9
24th April 1464 Battle of Hedgley Moor

	John Neville led the Yorkist army. ☺
Somerset fought against the Yorkists. The Lancastrian army was led by Henry Beaufort.	

10 15th May 1464 Battle of Hexham	
(The final battle of the first phase of the Roses War.)	
✂	☺
Henry Beaufort led the army and was heavily defeated and fled to Scotland. Somerset was captured and executed. Henry VI fled once more. Margaret d'Anjou and her son, Edward, remained in France. Margaret Beaufort and Stafford still resided in **Bourne** as they had since Towton.	

Wars of the Roses Part 2

Despite the Yorkist victory, the tables were about to change once more.

Warwick, the 'Kingmaker' was negotiating a political marriage for Edward IV. Edward seemed to have a rather 'cavalier' attitude to life at this point. He enjoyed much frivolity and the company of women; he already had several illegitimate children.

Warwick's choice of bride for Edward was to Louis XI's sister-in-law, 'Bona of Savoy'. However, Warwick was furious to learn that, despite his political wrangling, Edward had already married Elizabeth Woodville (Wydeville) who was a widow, a mother of two sons and of no political use whatsoever.

She was the daughter of Sir Richard Wydeville and her mother, Jaquetta of Luxembourg, the widow of John, Duke of Bedford. Jaquetta was often regarded as a witch with supernatural powers but not only this, Jaquetta was a very close friend of Margaret d'Anjou.

Edward had been impressed by Elizabeth's beauty and chastity as she had resisted his advances, even though he had held a dagger to her neck to get her to submit to 'his charms'.

Their marriage took place in secret and was attended only by her mother, a priest and two gentlewomen. Edward's mother, Cecily Neville, was so angry that she suggested he was illegitimate to allow another son to ascend to the throne Not only this but it was generally accepted that Edward had indulged in a similar previous secret marriage to Lady Eleanor Talbot.

A quote from the Milanese Ambassador at the time commented that the wedding had 'greatly offended the people of England'.[31] Margaret Beaufort was apparently horrified that she would have to be subservient to a commoner.

At this time, Henry VI was captured and taken to the Tower and had endured the indignity of being paraded through the streets wearing a straw hat. He was 'without all honour like a thief or an outlaw' being jeered by the people as he passed.

For the next five years, Margaret d'Anjou stayed in France trying to rally support and troops.

Margaret Beaufort and Stafford lived in relative safety in the Yorkist 'camp' and spent much of their time in Woking which had become their favourite property. It had once belonged to Edward the Confessor and had become a Holland residence. Margaret Holland inherited the property and had married Margaret's grandfather, John Beaufort I.

---

[31] https://books.google.co.uk Milanese Ambassador

The property was managed by Reginald Bray who remained a close friend of Margaret Beaufort throughout her life.

They enjoyed a peaceful life there with fifty servants and spent much time hunting, playing chess, cards and gambling.

In 1465, Margaret and her mother made a visit to Crowland. At Christmas 1466, her mother, the Duchess of Somerset, invited both Margaret and her husband for a stay of six weeks in Maxey which was, 'A convenient distance from their house in Bourne'.[32]

Meanwhile, William Herbert had a victory in Harlech Castle and so Henry (VII)'s keeper was made the Earl of Pembroke, the title once belonging to his uncle Jasper.

Margaret was granted a rare reunion with Henry (VII) at this time in Raglan Castle.

11
1467 Siege of Harlech Castle

Jasper wanted to recover his title and lands and he came with 'armed ships' and entered Wales. His money and the fleet had been supplied by Louis XI. Louis, seeking revenge, had probably been inclined to help Jasper because Edward IV had failed to marry his relation. Also, he was no doubt, encouraged by Margaret d'Anjou, who was still looking to reinstate Henry VI as King of England.

---

[32] N. Tallis quoting 'Crowland Chronicles'

12 **Seizure of Denbigh Castle 1468**	
Jasper's attempt to regain his title was unsuccessful but it did reignite the animosity between the houses of York and Lancaster.	
	The rift between Warwick and Edward deepened because of his unpopular marriage. Warwick
Warwick In 1469, Warwick and Edward's brother, George the Duke of Clarence, went to France together. On the 11th July, Warwick married his elder daughter, Isabelle to George, Duke of Clarence. Should they usurp Edward's throne, Warwick's daughter would become Queen as George would be the next in line for the throne. He hated the Woodville family who were all making prestigious marriages thanks to Elizabeth's ambitions to stay on the throne. Warwick and the Duke of Clarence sailed to England to depose Edward IV.	
	Edward IV was captured and sent to Warwick Castle. Baron Rivers, the Queen's father, and her son were executed. ☺

Margaret Beaufort and Stafford were at Weobly Castle, on the Gower Peninsular, home of Sir Walter Devereux and 150 miles away from the battles. However, they chose to travel to London to try to reinstate Henry (VII)'s birth-right. Sadly, William Herbert's wife, Anne had no intention of relinquishing power or lands and refused their petition. Margaret Beaufort was very disappointed. 👆		
	In July 1469, Warwick now attempted to rule but the barons did not support him. Warwick found himself so unpopular that he found it too difficult to rule and so he felt compelled to release Edward IV.	
		Edward forgave Clarence and Warwick and tried to establish peace but he was far more suspicious of their loyalty.

	Warwick and Clarence did indeed start to plot again, and this time with none other than Margaret Beaufort's stepbrother, Richard Welles. They started to raise troops in Lincolnshire.	

13
12th March 1470 Battle of Stamford/Empingham/ Losecoat Field.

Richard and Robert Welles ☞ ☞ ☞ ☞	Warwick, along with Robert and Richard Wells, fought against Edward IV for his crown. They were defeated and the 'Lancastrians' fled the battlefield throwing off their coats in order to run into the woods faster for their escape. The battle took place in Horn Field now named, 'Bloody Oaks'. Clarence and Warwick escaped to France and the Welles brothers were executed. ✂ ☹	

50

	Stafford joined the King at Stamford, but subsequently, it was his sad duty to ride to Maxey to tell Margaret Beaufort's mother that her sons had been killed.
It would seem that Margaret's mother, Margaret Beauchamp, had been involved in the plot against Edward IV. Where Margaret Beaufort stood with these divided loyalties, is unclear. What a difficult choice to make but, as was the pattern of her life, divided loyalties meant that at least someone in the family was going to remain in favour with the victor. This policy saved her life at times. Edward IV did pardon Margaret Beauchamp, possibly because Stafford had remained loyal. Warwick decided to ally with the Lancastrians.	

Henry VI and Margaret d'Anjou realised the only way to reinstate Henry to the throne was to accept Warwick the Kingmaker's assistance in taking the power of the throne away from Edward IV. Clarence and Warwick fled to France where they made a truce with Margaret d'Anjou and arranged the marriage of Warwick's second daughter, Anne Neville, to Edward, son of Henry VI. Warwick returned to England in 1471 with sixty ships and prepared for the invasion. Jasper Tudor joined Clarence and Warwick bringing with him troops from Wales, hoping to regain his lands and title.	
	Edward IV canvassed for support to match the troops of his treacherous brother and Warwick. He was not popular now, mainly because of the power-seeking Woodvilles. Edward had little choice but to flee to Flanders with his faithful brother, Richard (III), Lord Hastings and the Queen's brother, on 2nd October 1470, departing from Kings Lynn.

Warwick had 'practically the whole of the island was in his power'[33]. He went to Westminster and was met with joy; he proceeded to the Tower and released Henry VI. This period was known as the 'Readeption'. Henry, however, was in a confused state and so Warwick acted in the role of king but was Chief Minister in name. It was at this period that, unsurprisingly, Warwick became known as 'the Kingmaker'.	
	Commynes observed that 'Edward IV was a desperate man.' He had no money and 'there never was such a beggarly company'.[34] On a positive note, Edward's heir, Edward (V) was born on 2nd November 1470. The Queen gave birth in Westminster Abbey where she had taken her family into sanctuary for their safety.

---

[33] N. Tallis

[34] N. Tallis 'Commynes Memoires'

November 1470, Jasper took Henry (VII) to London. He was now 14 years old and Margaret Beaufort managed another brief meeting with him at Westminster. Here he was presented to Henry VI, possibly for the first time, when the King reputedly prophesied that Henry (VII) would one day be King.

The story has been questioned but should it have been true, there is no doubt that Margaret Beaufort would have seen this as a real possibility and it would have fired her enthusiasm to try to make this happen even though, prior to this, he had never been regarded as a serious contender to the throne.

In later years, the Tudors called this, 'a divine prophecy'.

Margaret Beaufort was reunited with her son, Henry (VII) in Woking, although he was still in Jasper's custody. Jasper regained his Earldom in Pembroke and the Duke of Clarence obtained a position in Henry VI's council.

Margaret Beaufort was feeling more secure from this recent turn of events and once more petitioned to get Henry's title and lands restored. Sadly, her request was denied, and she was disappointed once more.	
14th December 1470, Margaret d'Anjou, Edward and Anne Neville obviously felt more confident and chose to return to England.	
	In 1471, Edward IV was also planning to return to England arriving in Ravenspur on 14th March. He was joined by the Duke of Burgundy and two thousand men. Edward welcomed and forgave him, meeting him in Banbury.
George, Duke of Clarence once more swapped sides Warwick was furious at Clarence's defection. On the 24th March, the Queen, Edward and Anne Neville set sail for France.	George, Duke of Clarence

	Edward IV asked Margaret Beaufort's husband, Stafford, to join him but in the true fashion of Margaret's husbands, he was undecided.
	Edward arrived triumphantly in London and declared that Henry VI was deposed. Then, he went to Westminster Abbey to release his family from sanctuary and to greet his five-month old heir.
Henry Stafford decided to join Edward, despite his unpopularity with the Lancastrians. ☞ ☞ ☞ ☞ ☞	Gaining this support on 12th April, Edward resolved to crush the Lancastrians once and for all.

14
14th April 1471 Battle of Barnet

This battle was very bitter and was fought in mist and fog. The Lancastrians, led by Warwick, became confused by the lack of visibility and began attacking each other.

| | Edward had a good army and outnumbered Warwick's troops.

✂☺ |

Warwick was killed and his brother was knocked from his horse. Henry VI was taken prisoner and taken to the Tower. Margaret Beaufort received no word about her husband, Stafford, and was obviously so anxious that she travelled to London to search for news. She found Stafford, who was alive, but very badly injured and he never really recovered from these injuries. They returned to Woking to give him time for convalescence. Margaret d'Anjou sailed for England with more troops but experienced a dreadful crossing, so much so, that she contemplated returning to France, especially when she learned that Henry VI had been captured. However, Jasper reassured her that they had a chance of success and persuaded the royal party to land in England.	
	Edward IV discovered that she had landed and immediately wanted to capture Margaret d'Anjou.

30th April, the Lancastrians marched to meet Edward in battle. They reached Gloucester but the gates of the city were closed to them, forcing them to continue on to Tewkesbury on 3rd May.	

15
4th May 1471 Battle of Tewkesbury

Again, this was one of the bloodiest battles of the Wars of the Roses.

The Lancastrians were losing heavily and many, including Somerset, sought refuge in the Abbey. However, Edward's men were so ruthless that they dragged them out and slaughtered them. Somerset was executed in the marketplace on 6th May. Margaret d'Anjou's son, Edward, was killed in the battle.	Edward IV had a resounding victory. Margaret d'Anjou and Anne Neville were captured in 'Little Malvern Priory', Worcester. The Queen was devastated at losing her son and regarded this as the end of the Lancastrians.

Comynes commented 'that in eleven days, Warwick had won all England … In 21 days, King Edward had reconquered it though there were two desperate and bloody battles'[35]

---

[35] N. Tallis 'Commynes Memoires'

Margaret Beaufort would have felt totally crushed, Edward IV had regained the throne and also had a son and heir.

Any thoughts that her son, Henry, might one day be king must have been completely dashed. Stafford, who appears to have been a good husband, was failing in strength and she would be without a protector should he die.

Not only this but her son would be regarded as a great threat to the stability of Edward IV's throne and therefore, would be in a more vulnerable position than ever before. Margaret, indeed, was now the most senior female in the Beaufort family so putting Henry (VII) at risk.

❦

The next disaster to strike was that Henry VI was murdered in the Tower, possibly being suffocated with his pillow. It was suggested that either Edward IV or Richard (III) may have been responsible but others suggest he may have died of a broken heart.

❦

Jasper and Henry (VII) fled to Pembroke fearing for their lives. Margaret Beaufort was relieved at their escape and supported them in fleeing to France.

They departed from Tenby but the weather was so bad that they had to land in Brittany.

Duke Francis II welcomed them and looked after them suitably but in effect, they had become his prisoners.

Margaret Beaufort, now at the age of 28 years, not only saw her closest allies depart but more significantly, Stafford, her third husband, died.

Her close friend, Bray, who managed her estates, arranged the burial of her husband on her behalf.

🖐 🖐 🖐 🖐 🖐

Not being a woman to leave herself unprotected, she decided that she must marry again and chose Thomas Stanley to be her fourth husband. They married in June 1472, less than a year after Stafford's death. This was a very clever choice because

although Stanley was a Lancastrian at heart, he, like Stafford before him, allied himself to the Yorkists and so he too dithered 'on the fence' as to which side to support. ☞ ☞ ☞ ☞	
	Stanley had not supported Edward at Tewkesbury, but Edward forgave him and appointed him 'Steward of the King's Household'. Possibly Edward was generous because Thomas's brother, William, did fight by Edward's side. The brothers often seemed to split their allegiance which usually protected the other on the 'wrong side'.
In 1482, things looked brighter for Margaret Beaufort as Stanley seemed to be respected on the Yorkist 'side'. She must have been feeling far more confident as she began to petition, once more, for the restoration of Henry (VII)'s titles and lands.	

	Edward wanted to invade France and in 1475 began to make preparations.
	In July, he crossed the English Channel, but Louis XI was prepared to sign a peace treaty to avert war, with the promise that Edward's daughter, Elizabeth of York, would marry the Dauphin.
	They agreed to a 7-year truce. It would seem that Edward still feared the possibility of Henry (VII)'s return to claim the throne and so sent agents to Brittany asking Louis to hand him over. The incentive offered to Henry was that he would find him a suitable English wife, perhaps even one of his daughters.
Margaret Beaufort, playing her political card, now joined the Yorkist side. ☞ ☞ ☞ ☞ ☞ ☞ ☞	

	Margaret Beaufort was accepted into the House of York and had even become quite fond of Edward's children. She had accompanied the Queen and her daughters to Fotheringhay. However, Duke Francis was becoming weary of Edward's demands to release Henry (VII) and agreed to return him to England.
	Margaret became aware of this arrangement and sent word to Henry to warn him of the plot. When the time came, Henry said he was too ill to travel. Instead, he went into sanctuary in the Cathedral of St Malo.
	The English contingent tried to capture him but the townsfolk drove them away so saving Henry. Duke Francis realised the danger Henry faced and took him under his protection once more.

Henry (VII) went to Vannes and reunited with Jasper. Meanwhile, Richard (III) married Anne Neville, the widow of Margaret d'Anjou's son, Edward. This drove a wedge between the two brothers, the Duke of Clarence and Duke of Gloucester because as Anne was the sister of Clarence's wife Isabelle, this in effect halved the inheritance he would gain from the Warwick legacy.

The Duke of Clarence's Isabelle died in childbirth and consequently he decided to marry Mary of Burgundy. Edward thwarted this plot driving the brothers further apart.

In 1478, George, Duke of Clarence was accused of treason and executed. He chose to drown in a vat of malmsey maybe thinking Edward just wished to teach him a lesson.

Edward now had two sons, Edward (V) and Richard, Duke of York. Feeling more secure on the throne, he invited Henry (VII) back to England, even granting him £400 from his recently demised grandmother.

Edward IV became furious to find that the Dauphin was to marry Maximillian's daughter, thus 'dumping' Elizabeth of York' his daughter, and so breaking 'The Truce'.

Edward declared war on France, but before this came to pass he died, in April 1483, aged forty years.

Margaret Beaufort was most disappointed as she felt that, at last, Henry's birth-right was about to be restored. She was not confident with the new order as to whether this would come to fruition. Edward was buried in St George's Chapel, Windsor, as yet incomplete, but would, in the future, bear the symbol portcullis of the Beaufort/Tudor dynasty. Edward had appointed his brother, Richard (III) to be his son's regent, the boy being only 12 years of age.

Edward IV must have trusted his brother, Richard of Gloucester to honour his son's legacy. Richard (III) was born in Fotheringhay Castle on 2nd October 1452 and unlike his other brother, George, Duke of Clarence, he had always fought loyally in battle beside his older brother.

Elizabeth Woodville was not happy with this choice and wanted the power to remain firmly within her own household. She decided to take custody of her sons as soon as possible and to proceed with all haste to get Edward (V) crowned.

He was sent to London with Earl Rivers (Elizabeth's brother) and son, Richard Gray, on 24th April; the coronation was scheduled for 4th May.

Obviously being wary of Richard (III), she had not informed him of Edward's death, so giving her more time to secure Edward (V)'s coronation but certainly showing a disrespect for Richard.

Margaret was annoyed with Richard (III) as her husband had not been elevated to any higher rank in the royal household.	Elizabeth Woodville was incensed that Edward's guards had been locked in their rooms overnight and her son had been abducted. The guards, both her relations, were executed and Richard (III) had her son under his control.

| | Hastings had told Richard (III) that Edward (IV) had died. He hated the Woodvilles for their power as they had forced him to marry Elizabeth's sister, apparently a very unsuccessful union. |
| | He told Richard that he needed to act quickly to prevent them from establishing the royal family exclusively as their own. He was involved in the plot to 'kidnap' Edward (V) on 29th April. Richard said he was protecting her son, but Mancini said, 'the Duke had brought his nephew not under his care, but into his power, so to gain for himself the crown.'[36] |

---

[36] D. Mancini 'De Occupationne Regni Angeli per Riccardum Tercium' trans. And ed. As C A J Armstrong 'The Usurpation of Richard III (2nd edition, Oxford 1969)

Richard sent Edward (V) to the Tower, officially to await his coronation but no signs were apparent to indicate that this might take place. No new gowns or robes had been commissioned and no preparations were in evidence in Westminster Abbey.

It appears that Richard set about removing all his brother Edward's most trusted advisors. A tale seems to have been concocted that Hastings was going to attack him and, after a 'mock battle', Hastings was captured and beheaded in the Tower. There was no trial and it was regarded by many as an act of tyranny.

Margaret Beaufort would have been horrified by this especially as her husband, Thomas Stanley, had been imprisoned.

Possibly because his son, Lord Strange was a powerful man and would easily be able to command a large force against Richard, Stanley was released but decided it would be safer for him to swear his allegiance to Richard (III)

☞ ☞ ☞ ☞ ☞ ☞

Richard then proceeded to eliminate the next threat on his way to the throne by demanding that Elizabeth Woodville's other son be taken to the Tower.

The boys were once seen playing in the Tower gardens in summer 1483 but then never seen again. Their doctor was banned from seeing them even though Edward allegedly was having breathing problems.

In addition, the old argument arose that Edward's marriage to Elizabeth Woodville was not legal as he had already been married secretly before. The boys were then both deemed illegitimate, making Richard the 'only survivor of royal stock'.[37]

---

[37] E. Norton

Richard's ambition to take the throne now seemed to be more apparent as the coronation was moved to 22ⁿᵈ June.

Two days later, Richard was proclaimed King and his coronation took place on 7ᵗʰ July along with Anne Neville who became Queen, and both were magnificently dressed. Margaret Beaufort carried Anne's train and Stanley carried the mace, a clear indication to everyone that the House of Lancaster supported the new King.

	Richard III was becoming increasingly more unpopular.
Margaret Beaufort would now be even more afraid for her son, Henry (VII). All claimants to the throne had been eliminated except for him. Although Margaret Beaufort was still officially a trusted member in the York Family, she began to seriously plan for Henry to return and claim the throne for the Tudors. She seems to have been in a plot to rescue the Princes possibly because she would feel safer with Edward (V) on the throne.	Margaret Beaufort

	On discovering this plot, Richard ensured the boys were placed in a more secure place, deeper within the Tower. It is suggested they died shortly after this. Buckingham, one of Richard's close allies, now distanced himself from Richard and went to support Margaret Beaufort's 'side.
	❧ ❧ ❧ ❧ ❧ ❧
Buckingham, Humphrey Beaufort, himself a descendant of Edward III through his son, Thomas of Woodstock, probably saw that if Richard was deposed, he might have a claim to the throne himself. Margaret Beaufort, Bray, John Morton and Buckingham all wished to remove Richard III despite the next successor being undecided. Henry (VII)'s claim was still considered to be weak, especially as he had been out of the country for so long and nobody really knew much about him.	

To give more support to her plans, Margaret Beaufort made overtures to Elizabeth Woodville, who by now had really lost all her claims to be the Royal family. The two women agreed that it would suit them both if Henry (VII) and Elizabeth of York were to marry. Margaret now sent a message to Henry to set sail for England and claim the throne. This was her second plot to destabilise Richard III from the throne.	Elizabeth Woodville
	Richard's spies made the discovery of Margaret Beaufort's plans and warned him.
Elizabeth Woodville's son, the 'Marquess of Dorset' began to rally troops with the support of Edward Courtney, the Bishop of Exeter and Richard Guildford in Kent.	

16
18th October 1483 Battle of Rebellion

Buckingham went to Wales but the bad weather meant that he couldn't cross the River Severn.	
His men didn't like him, and they began to desert. He fled to France for his own safety. Dorset's men also began to desert, apparently because of the rain. Margaret Beaufort was devastated at this failure, partly for Henry, but she was now guilty of treason. Stanley … remained neutral! ✂ ☹ Although Buckingham had been unsuccessful, it did serve as a 'rallying point' and rebel groups began to form to fight against Richard III.	
	Richard realising his position was in danger from the new 'figure head', Henry (VII) He offered a reward for the capture of Buckingham.

	A servant of Buckingham betrayed him and he was captured and beheaded in Salisbury's marketplace on 2nd November.
	Richard III was furious with Margaret Beaufort, but Stanley avoided capture. Henry (VII), however, was now regarded as a traitor.
Henry (VII) was unaware of the failure of the rebellion but was still proceeding with his plans to journey to England and claim Elizabeth of York as his bride.	
He set off with forty ships and five thousand mercenaries on 12th October but the weather was so awful on the crossing, that his ships were scattered causing him to return to Brittany. (It has been suggested that this dreadful weather stopped this imminent battle and the delay in plans led to Henry's eventual success at Bosworth.)	

At this point, Margaret Beaufort should have been tried and executed for her treason but as Stanley had remained neutral and his powerful and influential brother, William, were of her family, they were able to protect her.

---

[38] E. Norton

Richard discovered that she had sent money to support this attack on his throne and sentenced her to life imprisonment but under the lock and key of her husband. Considering Richard's usual dealings with his rivals, Margaret had a very lucky escape! However, as Norton remarked, at the time she, 'was the focus of his wrath'.[38]	
Stanley did seem moved to help his wife and did seem to support her in efforts to help Henry despite his anger at her actions.	
It was a very low ebb for Margaret at this time. Her servant, Henry Parker, remarked that 'she was often in jeopardy of her life, yet she bare patiently all trouble'.[39]	

👆👆

	Richard III, now realising the full potential of the threat from Henry (VII) and of his growing popularity in Brittany, demanded that he should be extradited back to England. Stanley, being on the King's Council, learned of this plot and warned Margaret Beaufort of the imminent danger.
Henry (VII), received the warning from his mother and escaped from the Duke by disguising himself as a potter but the Breton soldiers were soon in pursuit.	
	Richard III devised a new plan. He offered Elizabeth Woodville the safety of his court if she joined him there and brought her daughters with her.

[39] Henry Parker quoted from Wikipedia (May 2020)

No doubt after all her years in sanctuary, a place at Court would have seemed very appealing and would give her daughters a chance of good marriages. ☞ ☞ ☞ ☞ ☞ ☞	
	At this point, it was suggested by his opponents, that Richard was intending to marry his niece, Elizabeth of York. This would be advantageous for two reasons. Firstly, it would consolidate his position as King as she was Edward IV's daughter and secondly, it would deprive Henry of his intended bride and weaken his claim to the throne. The difficulty of this suggestion was that his wife, Anne Neville, was still alive. Strangely she soon died and many thought Richard had killed her; she had been unable to give him another child and she was a sick woman. However, guilty or not, Richard lost so much popularity that he decided to say it was never his intention to marry Elizabeth of York. Elizabeth Woodville may have wished for this union, but the possible plot was abandoned.

Richard III was still very nervous about his position and decided that his next step would be to eliminate any possible opposition to his reign and so issued a proclamation against Jasper Tudor, the Bishop of Exeter, the Earl of Oxford and Edward Woodville calling them 'rebels and traitors.'[40]

Next, he revived the rumour, started by his mother, that Edward IV was illegitimate on both sides of his family.

He reiterated that Henry (VII) was from a bastard line, being a descendant from John of Gaunt's lineage from his union with Katherine Swynford and as such was barred from the succession.

Fearing the Stanley brothers' power, he imprisoned Lord Strange, Thomas Stafford's son, whom he threatened to execute should they rise up against him.

These moves made a great deal of discontent amongst the noble families and increasingly they became more convinced that Richard III was unfit to be King.

Henry (VII) was ready for the showdown. Charles VIII of France had granted him three to four thousand men, all of whom were a 'raggle taggle' mass of mercenaries but Henry managed to command their support.	
Jasper Tudor began to rally troops, including Rhys ap Thomas, the man who finally killed Richard III at Bosworth Field.	

---

[40] N. Tallis

	Richard III and Stanley met in Nottingham and progressed to Leicester together. Richard hoped this battle would finally rid him of all threats to his throne.

17
22th August Battle of Bosworth

Henry (VII), having successfully landed in Mill Bay, Milford Haven, Wales, progressed towards Leicester.	
	At the start of the battle, Richard sent in his archers. Richard killed Henry (VII)'s standard bearer, Sir William Brandon. The land was very marshy hindering the progress of his troops and probably, on seeing their troubles, Stanley finally committed to fighting on Henry (VII)'s side.
	In retaliation, Richard III ordered the beheading of Lord Strange, but the men refused to do this. The Earl of Northumberland betrayed Richard by remaining neutral in the battle. It was at this stage that Richard himself

	entered the battle and fought gallantly but his horse stumbled in the boggy marsh. He was killed in the battle, the last of the Plantagenet line. ✂
William Stanley's charge turned the battle in Henry's favour; Richard's Crown, reputedly found in a thorn bush, was retrieved and Thomas Stanley crowned Henry the 'King of England' whilst they were still on the battlefield. ☺☺☺☺☺☺☺☺	
	All of Richard's remaining supporters were executed. Richard had a very undignified entry into Leicester slung naked across the back of a horse.
It was reported by Bernard Andre, that Henry won by 'divine power'[41] as his army was much smaller than Richard's. Perhaps Margaret Beaufort's prayers were the deciding factor!	

---

[41] Bernard Andre (trans. Daniel Hobbins) 'The Life of Henry VII' (1500 – 1502; trans. 2016)

Generously, Henry paid for a tomb for Richard, costing £6,700 - a far cry from the car park in which he was found in the 21st century. Henry, in gratitude to his mother's continued support, gave her Richard's 'Book of Hours'; he erased Richard's name and wrote in his own.	

Margaret's desperate times in Richard III's reign, showed her extreme courage and showed what a survivor she truly was.

Nicola Tallis commented that, 'her determination to support her son confirms that she was a strong-minded woman who was prepared to risk her own safety in order to try to secure his (Henry's) future'.[42]

Now Henry VII, with his mother's continued support, went on to create one of the most famous dynasties in English history.

However, Henry's reign was not without opposition and yet one more battle had to be fought.

18
16th June 1487 Battle of Stoke Field

	A last try by the Yorkists to overthrow the Lancastrians, with Lambert Simnel as the figurehead, was led by John De La Pole, (Margaret Beaufort's first husband) and Colonel

---

[42] N. Tallis

	Martin Schwartz, with an army of eight thousand men, who were mostly Irish and Swiss/German mercenaries. ✂
Henry was supported by Lord Strange and George Stanley. As the Irish archers had only poor armour, the battle was soon won. ☺	

The Tudor Dynasty was at last established. It was extraordinary that Henry should have risen to the position of King when so many other claimants could easily have established themselves before him in the line of succession.

A final word from the great John Fisher stated, 'Having always found strength in her faith... she left behind her a dynasty that would be the most talked of in British history ... risking her life in the process.'[43]

---

[43] N. Tallis quoting John Fisher

5

'My Lady the King's Mother'

October 30th 1485, was Margaret's proudest day as she saw her son crowned 'Henry VII, King of England'. She must have thought that all their troubles were over (at least for the day). Being an astute woman, she would not have 'rested on her laurels' and she would have been right to stay alert to further threats to his throne. Fisher commented that Margaret wept with joy and fear, 'Her tears were a mixture of the greatest pride and fear.'[44]

Margaret's life was far from easy, with threats from pretenders claiming to be Richard, the younger brother of Edward V but also from the deaths of her closest friends and family.

Her achievements, however, were great. Henry trusted her like no other and relied heavily on her sound counsel for the enrichment of England and also for securing good political marriages within the Tudor family.

---

[44] John Fisher 'Mornynge Remembrance' through Early English Books online (2020)

Nicola Tallis stated that, 'Margaret had been in among the action, watching political manoeuvrings as kings and queens lost and gained the throne. She had played her hand expertly, and as Henry's reign progressed, her strategies would prove to be just as shrewd.'[45] This was so much so that the Spanish Ambassador felt that she was the greatest influence in England throughout Henry's reign.

One of the most serious threats to Henry VII's throne was that of a pretender called, Perkin Warbeck. The arrival of this pretender also threatened the marriage plans for his son, Arthur, to Katherine of Aragon, a political move to secure an alliance with Spain.

Margaret would have been in a central position in this very real threat to Henry's throne. Perkin's claim was that he was the younger of the two Princes in the Tower and theoretically was therefore Richard IV. It was a very strong claim at the time, supported by several foreign royal families and his claim has still not been completely discounted even today.

It is possible that this second son of Edward IV was not sent to the Tower to join his brother, Edward V. Richard III threatened to use force to extricate the boy from his mother, Elizabeth Woodville, who, already fearing Richard's ambition for the throne, had hastily taken her children into the sanctuary of Westminster Abbey.

She had good reason to be so cautious, knowing that Richard had already 'captured' her elder son. He had previously executed her son from her first marriage, Richard Grey, and also her brother, Lord Rivers, when they were acting as Edward's escorts to London for his coronation.

---

[45] N. Tallis

Elizabeth was an astute woman and as the wife of Edward IV, had always had to fight for her right to be Queen. This had made her unpopular as she tended to secure her position by arranging the marriages of those eligible in her family to nobles of the main families in England. She had the continued fight to prove the legitimacy of her children as many believed and indeed stated openly that Edward IV had been married secretly to Eleanor Talbot before his marriage to her. It was her marriage to Edward, that caused the rift between him and Warwick 'the Kingmaker'.

Knowing of her shrewd nature, this raises the question as to whether she would give up her younger son to Richard III, as he would be the only security left to her, in order for her to regain her royal position.

It is possible that, like all mothers, she would try to save him from disaster. It has been suggested that a substitute was sent in his place. There would, after all, be few people who could verify his authenticity; there were no photographs, social media or other technological methods to prove that they had the right boy.

Now Warbeck had returned and set about reclaiming his alleged throne. What a dreadful position for Margaret to be placed in. If the pretender was genuine, his claim to the throne was far stronger than Henry's.

One would think his mother and sister would recognise him or at least verify his authenticity, but would they want to? Time had moved on! Elizabeth of York was the Queen and her son, Arthur, was to be the next 'King of England'. Would this have been more prestigious than being the sister of the King?

For Elizabeth Woodville, in confirming Warbeck's identity as genuine, she could be condemning her own daughter to relative obscurity and worse, deny the throne to her grandson.

However, before Warbeck had made his claim, an earlier pretender, Lambert Simnel, declared that he was Richard and so such a challenge was not new but the threat of Warbeck would not go away.

He claimed that he had been secreted away from Westminster by a boatman and taken to safety. His story was certainly endorsed by the Duchess of Burgundy in November 1492; she declared that Warbeck was a genuine claimant to the throne even though she had only met him once before on a visit to England when he was a young boy. She did, however, have a personal grudge from the past with Henry VII, so here was a perfect opportunity to depose him.

Warbeck tried to gain support from Queen Isabella of Spain but she had little to gain from this as plans were already in place for her daughter, Katherine of Aragon, to marry Henry VII's son, Arthur, and thus he failed to raise support for his cause from Spain.

Unfortunately, especially for Margaret Beaufort, he was more successful in Scotland; they were far more convinced with his authenticity and he was allowed to marry Lady Katherine Gordon, who just happened to be James IV's cousin and consequently now related to Margaret Beaufort's granddaughter, Margaret.

If Warbeck was genuine, as the second son of the King, his title would be 'Duke of York'. Therefore, in order to clarify the stance of the Tutor family on this point, Margaret Beaufort accompanied Henry VII and Elizabeth of York to Westminster Abbey where Henry (VIII), their second son, was officially awarded the title of 'Duke of York' (a title that to this day is given to the monarch's second son).

Margaret dressed 'magnificently for the occasion and wore her coronet' indicating there would be no doubt as to her position on this issue. There were three days of celebration which included very public jousts; a very forceful statement had been made.

However, the horror of this situation with Warbeck continued, as her brother-in-law, William Stanley (who, by his actions at Bosworth, helped to decide the outcome of the battle) was a supporter of Warbeck's claim! Margaret must have been in total shock at this turn of events; William Stanley was a man of standing and had proved that he could command strong forces when needed.

With little option, Henry VII had Stanley arrested, taken to the Tower and executed on 16th February 1495.

This unforeseen turn of events hit Margaret at one of her lowest points. Not only this but her three-year-old granddaughter (daughter of Henry VII) died on 14th September 1495. Then, on 21st December, the great protector for herself and Henry, Jasper Tudor, died. He had been a constant in her life and had taken care of Henry in his years of exile and was of course, her brother-in-law.

At least she still had Henry VII and Elizabeth of York to comfort her and they travelled to Corfe Castle which had been restored to her ownership (it had once been a castle owned by her father) and she set about its aggrandisement.

By the summer of 1497, the threat from Warbeck grew; he had raised more troops and was strengthened further by the men of Cornwall, who were aggrieved at the amount of taxes they had to pay Henry VII and also because he had closed their, 'Stannary Parliament'.

In response to this serious threat, Elizabeth of York and the royal family retreated to the safety of the Tower, 'Nobel men from across England rushed to London with their own soldiers to defend the king from the Cornish. Before long, the King's army had grown to 25.000 men. At this time, this was one of the largest armies ever gathered by a king of England.'[46]

The uprising culminated at the Battle of Blackheath, when Oxford, Baron Daubenary, defeated the rebel army resulting in the deaths of a thousand or more Cornishmen. Their leaders, Michael Joseph An Gof and Thomas Flamank were hung, drawn, and quartered.

Now, Isabella and Ferdinand of Spain were more confident in the security of the Tudor claim to the throne and allowed the official betrothal of Katherine to Arthur; he was ten years old and she was just a year older.

On 17th September, Warbeck instigated a second rebellion in Exeter but support for him was now waning and on 5th October, he surrendered and was taken to the Tower. Probably in fear of his life, he admitted that his claim was false, and probably was hoping for the same leniency of the previous pretender, Lambert Simnel, who had been set to work in the royal kitchens and later rose to a higher office.

Margaret must have been feeling slightly more secure and she and the royal party went to stay at Collyweston.

Meanwhile, Warbeck escaped with the collusion of another prisoner, the Earl of Warwick, none other than the son of George, Duke of Clarence who strangely or deliberately was imprisoned next to Warbeck's cell.

This conveniently gave Henry a reason to have them executed. Warbeck was recaptured and by November both prisoners were put on trial, found guilty of treason and sentenced to death.

---

[46] E. Norton

As a Plantagenet, and the son of Edward IV's brother, Warwick's claim to the throne could have been argued to be far stronger than Henry VII's but by these executions, the last serious challengers to his throne had been eliminated.

The executions took place on 23rd November 1499 by hanging and then beheading, after which their heads were displayed on spikes outside the Tower.

Now permission was given to Katherine by her parents to travel to England to marry Arthur, a pleasing outcome, but Katherine always felt that her marriage was 'made in blood'.[47]

Margaret's joy and happiness were marred once more as her favourite grandson, Edmund died at the age of one year old.

Now, she spent much of her time in Collyweston, overseeing the improvements and refurbishments but she still continued with her royal duties.

Margaret had been a useful advisor to her daughter-in-law and although many accounts of their relationship suggest that Margaret was overbearing, she did seem to have a kindly and helpful relationship with her. For example, when Katherine arrived in England, Margaret gave her two very sound pieces of advice; the first was to learn French so that she could understand and be understood in the English court and the second was to drink wine, as the water in England was so unhealthy.

When Katherine had first arrived in England, she had just experienced a very difficult sea journey. She had arrived with a large Spanish retinue and was taken to Dogmersfield, in Hampshire

---

[47] Wikipedia (May 2020)

on 2nd October, where she met Arthur for the first time. She was now fifteen years old and Arthur was fourteen.

The whole royal court proceeded to London for the splendid festivities surrounding their wedding; Margaret Beaufort was in attendance, accompanied by two of her granddaughters.

The wedding took place in old St Paul's Cathedral on 14th November 1501, thus cementing a strong alliance with the Spanish court.

Interestingly, Arthur and Katherine were put to bed together that night as was expected. Both were physically mature, and they seemed to be genuinely fond of each other. It was usual to inspect the sheets in the morning!

In later years, this was rather important when Katherine of Aragon denied that the marriage had been consummated whilst Henry VIII was trying to find reasons to divorce her. Compared to Margaret Beaufort, who had given birth to Henry when she was only thirteen, the question of 'innocent or not' in her claims would have been ridiculed at the time. The most important 'job' of a royal bride was to produce an heir, and therefore any reluctance to perform her duties would have been most odd. (There again, they were only teenagers!)

Margaret invited the newly-weds to another of her houses, Coldharbour in London, and again feted them with lavish entertainments.

Margaret Beaufort continued arranging the unions for the royal family. She was instrumental in making the arrangements for her granddaughter Margaret, in her betrothal to James IV of Scotland.

The betrothal took place when Margaret was just twelve years old but Margaret Beaufort, being mindful of her unpleasant, early marital experiences and of her difficult experience of childbirth, would not let the marriage take place until her granddaughter was more physically mature.

Eventually the pair were married on 8th August 1503 but such was Margaret's authority that she could delay this event until she thought fit.

Margaret's contentment was, once more, short lived. She received the most shattering news that Arthur had died following a sickness, possibly tuberculosis, at Ludlow Castle. This dreadful event occurred only five months after he had been married to Katherine.

What a dreadful state of affairs! Arthur, who had been trained from birth to be a king, was gone, leaving the stability of the Tudor dynasty in tatters and a daughter-in-law without any real place in the Court, having not yet produced an heir.

This threw Margaret into despair and Henry VII and Elizabeth of York decided they must try to produce another heir before her child-bearing years were over.

Margaret was left to turn her attention to the Duke of York, Henry (VIII), to try to prepare him to step into his brother's shoes.

Margaret regarded him as a frivolous young man who spent his time on his own entertainment, rather than on any thoughts of how to rule a country. She faced such real challenge here as she also struggled with the signs of her approaching old age. She worried about him not being a suitable heir and feared greatly that he would turn away from the church. She sounds quite a prophetess!

Sadly, the new son that Henry and Elizabeth had hoped for was in fact a daughter. The strain of childbirth was obviously too much for Elizabeth, who developed puerperal fever. On 11th February, her thirty seventh birthday, Elizabeth of York died, followed quickly by her new-born daughter, Katherine, just seven days later.

At this point, Margaret became the most senior female in the royal family and remained so until her death in 1510. Henry had thought of remarrying, one candidate being his son's widow, Katherine of Aragon, but none of these plans came to fruition.

Margaret kept in touch with her granddaughter, Margaret, in Scotland, and was delighted to hear of the birth of their heir, James, on 21st February 1502. She was crushed again when the infant died.

Shortly after this, her husband, Stanley, died on 29th July 1504. She may not have had a close relationship in physical terms but they had enjoyed a close relationship on perhaps a more business-like level and Margaret must have started to feel very alone at this point.

She was very independent, however, no longer needing the protection of a husband as she was remarkably wealthy. This, at least, would have given her a feeling of security and she was able to conduct herself in 'a queenly manner for the entirety of the rest of her life'.[48]

Henry would never trust anyone to advise him better than his mother and, as Nicola Tallis points out, she had 'earned the utmost respect and admiration of those on her son's council at court' and for the first time, Margaret was officially recognised in her role as, 'uncrowned queen''.

Henry, despite claiming her residence at Woking for himself (not welcomed by Margaret) did endow her with many other properties. Not only this, he conferred on her the, 'Order of the Garter', the first woman to be included in the traditional twenty-four aristocratic members.

---

[48] N. Tallis

When Henry VII's heirs were born, it was Margaret who had organised the birthing room, following the strictest etiquette and indeed she was present at the birth of the future, Henry VIII. (This etiquette was adopted by Margaret, her granddaughter, whilst giving birth to the future King of Scotland, James V).

Henry VII honoured her, by naming his first daughter Margaret after her.

The worst trauma of Margaret's life came, however, in 1509 on 21st April at Richmond Palace, when Henry died at 11pm. He had been ill for some time and his eyesight had been failing. His death seemed to be very troubled. John Fisher talked 'of this man in agony, not for the dread of death only but for the judgement of almighty God'.[49]

Certainly, he would have been responsible for the deaths of many men, but battles and executions were quite the norm in those turbulent years. So was it the particular deaths of Warbeck (Richard) or perhaps the son of George, Duke of Gloucester, both challengers to his throne, that worried him? Was it perhaps the 'Princes in the Tower' after all, or was he simply pious and any deaths accountable to his soul were a burden? More mysteries that, at present, will go unsolved.

Despite this terrible blow, Margaret focussed on ensuring Henry (VIII) was to be crowned as the next King of England. However, Henry (VIII) was still only seventeen and would not inherit the Crown until his eighteenth birthday.

Somehow, she held on to her power in those two months until Henry came of age, thus securing the Tudor dynasty for which she had fought all her life. She did this, despite being heart-broken and

---

[49] N. Tallis

only surviving her son by two months, as she died on 29th June 1509.

Henry VIII was crowned King on 24th June 1509 attended by Margaret. However, she ate some cygnet at the coronation feast and, five days later, she was dead. Fisher remarked that 'All England for her death had cause of weeping.'[50]

Margaret, in spite of her original intention for her burial to be at Bourne Abbey, was interred at Westminster Abbey, a fitting place for such an amazing woman. She was laid to rest there on 3rd July on the south side of the Henry VII Chapel.

John Fisher of course gave the eulogy for her, saying that 'everyone who knew her loved her and everything she said or did became her'.[51]   In all, her funeral cost £680,000 (in today's money) which she had planned herself.

An iron grill surrounds the tomb, provided by St John's College, Cambridge, and was decorated by an Italian sculptor, Pietro Torrigiano. 'Her head rests on two pillows with a design of the portcullis and the Tudor rose...her wrinkled hands are raised in prayer'.[52]

In conclusion, the important question must be addressed:

Why she has been so overlooked in the local history of Bourne, Collyweston, Maxey and Deeping?

Even Shakespeare, writing during the reigns of Elizabeth I and James I, does not refer to her in name. His only reference comes in his play, 'Richard III', saying:

---

[50] N. Tallis quoting John Fisher
[51] N. Tallis quoting John Fisher
[52] N. Tallis

'Tell me how fares our loving mother
Who prays continually for Richmond's good?'[53]

My hope is that now we can appreciate what an amazing woman she was. She was highly respected during her lifetime and we should grant her the respect she deserves.

---

[53] W. Shakespeare 'Richard III' (1593)

6

Margaret's Symbols, the Portcullis and the Tudor Rose

When looking at the Angel Hotel in the Market Place in Bourne, above the main archway are two carvings set in the stones. On the left is a portcullis and on the right is the Tudor rose.

Knowing that Margaret lived in Bourne and enjoyed the trappings of her royal ancestors and that these were her very symbols, it is difficult not to conclude that these could have been embellishments on the castle itself even though they are set in a more 'modern' stone.

Margaret was already a wealthy woman when she lived in Bourne; she had an independent spirit, was fiercely proud of her Lancastrian heritage and her Tudor son. She always saw herself as an important woman who would have every reason to want to display the symbols of her house emblazoned on her castle.

The hotel was built in the late 17th century and certainly at a time when the castle had already fallen into disrepair, possibly after

Cromwell's men had left their encampment there in the civil war. Good stone was never wasted, and this may have been purchased by certain residents in Bourne in order to construct their own buildings.

Shippon Barn, The Well Head Cottage on the site of the castle and 'Stone House' in South Street are all reputed to have been built from the castle's stone. Indeed, 'Shippon Barn' exhibits crossbow slits today that definitely suggest evidence of a stone fortification from the past.

The owner of the site at the time of the castle's demolition was Lord Burghley of the Cecil family, Elizabeth I's Treasurer. (His son, Robert was of equal importance to Elizabeth I after his father William had fallen from favour having been instrumental in the execution of Mary Queen of Scots).

Lord William was born in Bourne in the manor that became a public house in later years, know firstly as 'The Bull Hotel' and later, in tribute to him, 'The Burghley Arms'.

This influential family would perhaps have distributed the castle stonework, probably for a fee but it would seem fitting that the castle embellishments should be preserved and used opposite William Cecil's birthplace and in the centre of the town.

Certainly, the portcullis here does not display the crown above it but during Margaret's residency in Bourne, she was not of the reigning royal family. Once Henry VII became King, she called herself 'The King's Mother' and adopted the crown symbol for herself. This can be seen in evidence on the entrance to St John's College Cambridge, a place where her patronage is well documented and where her portcullis is clearly displayed surmounted by a crown.

It has been pointed out that the Angel Hotel was at some point a tax office and consequently explains the existence of the portcullis there, but why the Tudor rose?

The portcullis was in fact the symbol of the Lancastrian family and adopted by Margaret's predecessor, John Beaufort I, the grandson of Edward III.

Edward III had been at war in France and he needed money to pay for these expenses. He therefore introduced a tax that had to be paid by everyone over the age of fifteen years. The symbol he chose for his tax collectors was the portcullis, representing the 'Gates of the Kingdom'. These gates were representative of the seaports and the symbol became that of the 'Customs and Excise'.[54]

When Edward III died, despite the fact that these taxes had made him very unpopular, his son, John of Gaunt continued to use this insignia. In order to give his family recognition from his relationship with Katherine Swynford, when their legitimacy was in question, he bequeathed this to his son, John Beaufort. This was used by all the Beaufort descendants and of course, came to Margaret as the only legitimate heir of her father and the Lancastrian House.

Henry VII subsequently adopted this symbol and used it so frequently that it can be seen today in so many places. It is used in the Palace of Westminster, King's College, Cambridge, St Stephen's Chapel and in St George's Chapel, Windsor. The portcullis, without the crown, has been associated with 'The City' since Tudor times. Edward the Confessor commissioned the building of Westminster Abbey during his reign of (1042–1066) but Henry VII began its rebuilding and improvements in his reign (1485-1509).

It is also included in the 'Dukes of Westminster of Beaufort's' family arms, the Westminster Bank (erstwhile), and the National Westminster Bank of today which continues to use the portcullis as its seal.

---

[54] Wikipedia (May 2020)

It has been disputed, that the portcullis was the design of Charles Barry in 1834 and used for many royal commissions such as can be seen on the Great Bell (Big Ben). Also, Elizabeth II gave a formal grant in 1996 for office use in Parliament.

The House of Commons Information Office, however, suggest that the portcullis symbol goes further back in our history of England, stating:

'The crowned portcullis has come to be accepted during the twentieth century as the emblem of both Houses of Parliament. As with many aspects of parliamentary life, this has arisen through custom and usage rather than as a result of any conscious decision.'[55]

'It was under the Tudors that The Palace of Westminster ceased to be the seat of the court and became the regular meeting place of Parliament'.[56]

One only need to look back at the stonework of Tudor England to see that this was the proud emblem of Margaret Beaufort's Lancastrian family.

In conclusion, it is possible to suggest that the decoration on 'The Angel Hotel' Bourne, is one of the earliest examples of the Beaufort use of their Lancastrian symbol of the portcullis. If this is disproved, there is still a wealth of places where her symbol is displayed. One of the best examples is in Henry VII's chapel in Westminster Abbey with its spectacular Pendant Fan Vault ceiling.

---

[55] House of Common Information Office
[56] House of Commons Information Office

Interestingly 'Perhaps the association of the rose, a symbol of beauty, and the portcullis, one of strength, may suggest a play or rebus (Beau-fort) on the Tudor family name.'[57]

<hr>

[57] Wikipedia (May 2020)

Illustrations

Figure 1: Margaret's symbols displayed on the archway of the Angel Hotel.

Figure 2: Reconstruction model of Bourne Castle in the making, by Steven Giullari.

Figure 3: Model of the round tower in situ on the Well Head
by Steven Giullari.

Figure 4: The Well Head showing the inner moat of the castle.

Figure 5: Stone House, allegedly built from the castle stone.

Figure 6: The Shippon Barn, allegedly built from the
castle stone, showing crossbow slits.

Figure 7: View of the Abbey Church across the Well Head
from the site of the round tower.

Figure 8: Collyweston Church, showing the building to the right,
where Margaret Beaufort was reported to pray.

Figure 9: The window Margaret Beaufort would look through to
join services within Collyweston church.

Figure 10: The sundial, possibly in Margaret Beaufort's garden in Collyweston.

Figure 11: The coat of arms of Bourne, based on the arms
of the Wake Family.

7

Bourne Castle

In writing about Bourne Castle, where Margaret Beaufort lived for five years with her husband, Henry Stafford, I shall be brief. There are far greater authorities on this subject and new facts are emerging all the time.

The most helpful guide, at present, is to access the' Bourne History Group' web page, established by Steven Giullari. He has entered photographs taken from a geophysical survey which clearly shows the layout of the castle, from a time when the land was parched. Not only this, he is making a model of the castle which is being completed as I write.

There have been archaeological excavations in the past. One was in 1861, and this led to a detailed plan of the castle being published; this has been accepted as the best plan until recently. Now, with modern technology, Steven Giullari has been able to add far more detail to the basic castle plan.

According to J.D. Birkbeck's research[58], the 1861 excavation did reveal the lower parts of two circular towers slightly west of the earthen mound. The walls must have been about three feet thick and placed 16 feet 6 inches apart. It would seem that these towers formed the gatehouse to the 'inner baily or courtyard'[59] in which stood the keep. Timbers were found 'in a sunken chamber near the "gatehouse"',[60] and these were thought to be 'part of the leverage for raising the drawbridge over the moat which surrounded the inner bailey'.[61] Opposite the gatehouse below the soil, were the remains of a wall that may have served as the support of the drawbridge when let down. If this was correct then the moat would be 44 feet in size.

The excavators realised that there was a second moat bounded by St Peter's Pool and the course of the Bourne Eau. Thus, the Keep was protected 'on the south side by a single moat and the other three sides by two moats'.[62] They agreed, on this excavation, that stones from the castle were visible on the Shippon Barn and agreed the stones and crossbow slits would have been part of the castle's round tower.

In 1889, the Lincolnshire and Nottingham Architectural Society confirmed the existence of one of the round towers, as this could be 'discernible'[63] but they agreed that the other tower must have existed.

In 1960, when the electricity board had to dig a trench across the field, a 'well preserved wall was revealed'.[64] Steven Giullari had

---

[58] J. D. Birkbeck 'A History of Bourne' (Jan 1976)
[59] J D Birkbeck (pp*)
[60] J. D. Birkbeck
[61] J. D. Birkbeck
[62] J. D. Birkbeck
[63] Lincolnshire and Nottingham Architectural Society
[64] J. D. Birkbeck

the good sense to take small samples of the stone for analysis in order to discern from which quarry this stone may have been taken.

We have been helping in this research; at first it was supposed that the stone had been quarried from Barnack. However, Steven Giullari had the stone analysed and our thoughts are, at present, that Collyweston or Witham are more likely. Stone was usually transported within a seven-mile radius of the buildings and these two quarries are fairly likely to be possible candidates.

As Steven points out, different types of stone would be used in the construction of different parts of the castle so it may be that the stone was accessed from more than one quarry.

This research is on-going, and more information will eventually be accesses on the 'Bourne History Group' web page.

In 2002, Channel 4's 'Time Team', with Tony Robinson, showed an interest in helping to discover more information but sadly objections at the time stopped this from taking place; perhaps the natural beauty of the Well Head could have been compromised.

Steven Giullari is able to identify the positions of other castle features. He has located the round tower which had commanding views of the fens, the dungeon, the porter's lodge, the kitchens, the castle walls, and the inner and outer moats.

Following the floods this year, in 2020, the indentations of the ground were filled with water providing a clear illustration of the inner moat in particular.

Again, from Steven Giullari's studies, he is able to make suggestions as to how the castle was defended by both the topography of the land and also the position of the buildings; it was a very secure Norman Castle.

Kenneth Jacob, a local historian, has looked at primary resources regarding the history of the castle. He has found that the earliest references were in 1179 – 1180, during Henry II's reign. For sure, Henry was a great castle builder and was certainly responsible for the building of Dover Castle although it is doubtful that he ever went there for a visit.[65] The only definite verification of dates for Bourne Castle would be if dateable artefacts were found in context.

The earliest recorded owners of the land of the castle were Leofric and Godiva, followed by their son, Aelfgar Earl of Mercia.

Then the lands fell to Lord Morcar (1067) who is recorded as fighting against the Normans with his relative, Hereward the Wake. The ownership then passed to William De Rollos, Lord of Bourne, in 1130 but as he had no children of his own, the property was inherited by his niece, Adelina de Rollos.

Adelina married Baldwin Fitzgilbert de Clare who is credited with building the stone castle and allegedly the Abbey Church. The castle was owned by the Wake family from that time.

There was a charter enacted by Blanche Wake of Liddell (1305 -1380), the wife of Thomas Wake, 2nd Baron Wake of Liddell, placing her at the castle, or at least owning it after her husband had died. Following her death, the castle passed to Joan, 'the Fair Maid of Kent', a fascinating woman who eventually became the mother of Richard II. The story of Joan would certainly make a 'best seller'.

Following her death, the castle went to the Holland family of her husband and finally, to his granddaughter, Margaret Holland who married John Beaufort I, the son of John of Gaunt.

---

[65] Kenneth Jacob (pp*)

Their son, John Beaufort II, married Margaret Beauchamp and together they became the parents of Margaret Beaufort. On her father's death, Margaret, as his only heir, inherited the lands and castle in Bourne. Had her father not taken his own life, he would have been executed for treason and his lands would probably have reverted to the Crown but by his actions, he at least secured his property for his child to inherit thus making Margaret one of the richest heiresses in England.

How history could have been different!

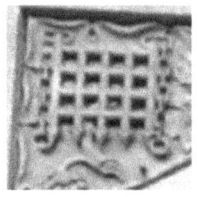

8

Castle Ownership

A. Richard the Fearless, 1st Duke of Normandy (943-996) + Emma of Paris Gunnor

B. Geoffrey Count de Brionne (996-1015) + Aubree Lasceline du Turqueville

C. Gilbert de Brionne (1000-1040) + Gunnora D'Aunou

D. Richard Fitzgilbert (1035-1090) 1st Lord of Clare + Rohese Giffard + Gunnor

E. Gilbert Fitz Richard de Clare (1066-1117) + Adeliza de Clermont

1. Leofric Lord of Mercia and Lady Godiva (975-1057)

2. Alfgar Earl of Mercia, Earl of East Anglia (1002-!063)

3. Earl Morcar (their son) (1044-1087) ally of Hereward the Wake

4. Hereward the Wake (1035-1072)

5. Oger the Breton (1096)

6. William de Rollos Lord of Bourne

7. 3rd son Baldwin Fitzgilbert de Clare (1092-1194) Lord of Bourne + Adeline de Rollos

8. Emma FitzGilbert de Clare (1114-1168) + Hugh Wac Ne'grevillea (1144)

9. Baldwin Wake I (1137-1198) + Agnes of Honnet

10. Baldwin Le Wac II (1184-1224) + Isabel de Briwere (1184-1233)

11. Hugh Wake (1212 – 1241) + Joan of Suteville (b 1219)

12. Baldwin Wake III (1236-1282) + Howise de Quincey

13. John Wake 1st Baron Wake of Liddell (1268 – 1300) + Joan Fibbernand Lady Joan Wake

14. Thomas Wake 2nd Baron Wake of Liddell (1268-1330) + Blanche (m1317)

15. (John's daughter) Margaret 3rd Baroness Wake (1305-1380) + Edmund Earl Of Woodstock (1301 – 1330)

16. Joan 'Fair Maid of Kent' Princess of Wales (1328 – 1385) + Thomas Holland 1st Earl of Kent (1314-1360) +_William Montagu + Edward Woodstock (Black Prince) (1330-1376)- (son Richard II)

17. Thomas Holland II Earl of Kent 1st Duke of Surrey (1350-1397) + Alice FitzAlan (1350-1416)

    (Thomas Holland 3rd Duke of Kent (1372-1400) + Joan Stafford)

18. Margaret de Holland de Beaufort (1385-1439) + John de Beaufort I (1373-1410)

19. John Beaufort II (1404-1444) + Margaret Beauchamp (1410-1482)

20. Margaret Beaufort (1443-1509) Countess of Richmond + (4 husbands)

    I. John De La Pole (1442-1492)
    II. Edmund Tudor (1430-1456)

III. Henry Stafford (1455-1483 (Duke of Buckingham)
IV. Thomas Stanley (1435-1456)

21. Henry VII (1457-1507)

22. Henry VIII (1491-1547)

23. Henry FitzRoy (1519-1536) (son of Henry VIII and Bessie Blount)

24. William Heckington de Bourne (1440-1587) + Alice Walcot (1454)

25. Lady Jane Heckington (1500-1588) + Richard Cecil (1495-1553)

26. William Cecil 1st Baron Burghley KG PC Lord High Treasurer of England (1520-1598) + Mary Cheke (d. 1543)

27. Robert Cecil 1st Earl of Salisbury KG PC Baron Cecil of Essendon, Viscount Cranborne (1563-1612) + Elizabeth Brooke

28. Bourne Urban Town Council

The Owners of the Castle Lands .... with a Few Juicy Bits!

1.   Leofric, Lord of Mercia and Lady Godiva

In Bourne, we are very proud of our heritage in that Leofric and Lady Godiva were early owners of the castle grounds so much so that we have a Leofric Avenue and a Godiva Crescent.

Leofric was a feudal Anglo-Saxon lord and was trying to extract far too much in taxes, or 'Heregeld', from his people. He was an all-powerful lord ruling England under the Danish King Canute. He tyrannised the church and had no respect for Godiva's religion nor for her lands.

Godiva, or 'Godifu', was unusual because only a very few women were landowners in England in the early 1100s and she owned much land in the Midlands. According to folk lore, Godiva pleaded with Leofric to reduce the crippling taxes that he imposed on his people but he retaliated by saying he would only reduce them if she rode through the streets naked.

Godiva then took this upon herself, for the sake of his tenants, to ride through the streets of Coventry on horseback, with only her long hair to preserve her modesty. The peoples of Coventry hid their eyes all except, 'Peeping Tom' who reputedly became blind after the event; it was suggested that this was a punishment from God.

The event apparently had a profound effect on Leofric. He joined Godiva in her religion and helped her to establish a Benedictine Priory in Coventry.

The first version of the story appeared 100 years later, written by Roger Windover and later recalled once more in a poem, 'Godiva', by Tennyson.

It sounds a wonderful piece of fiction, but the 'Historic' site suggest that it could possibly be true.

There are some wonderful pieces of art depicting the story of Godiva on her horse but there is also a depiction of Peeping Tom, in Coventry, in front of Coventry Cathedral Lane's shopping centre.

2. **Alfgar Earl Of Mercia Earl of East Anglia (1002 – 1063) (their Son) + Aelfgifu**

3. **Earl Morcar (their son) (1044-1087) ally of Hereward the Wake**
    Morcar fought alongside Hereward the Wake against the Normans. He was taken hostage by William the Conqueror in 1067, in Normandy and was imprisoned until his release in 1068 when he returned home.

    He organised another rebellion against William along with support from the English and Welsh monks, the clergy and the poor.

    This also failed and he was again captured but he escaped in 1070. Hereward held the Isle of Ely against the Norman rule but when Hereward was crushed, Morcar surrendered.

Sadly, Edwin, his brother, who was also involved in the plot was betrayed and killed. Morcar was imprisoned once again but when William was on his deathbed, he ordered the release of Morcar. He returned home but William Rufus, William I's successor, imprisoned him in Winchester where he probably died.

4.   **Hereward the Wake (1035-1072)**

Charles Kingsley placed Hereward firmly in Bourne and we boast of a Hereward Street, Hereward Lodge, a Wake's football team, our two secondary schools have divided his heraldic badge between them, and the town has adopted his motto,'Vigila et Ora', 'Watch and Pray'.

Hereward, an Anglo-Saxon nobleman, was a leader against the invasion of the Normans following their conquest in 1066; he was allegedly the uncle of Morcar and his brother, Edwin.

He was a great leader but rather a hot-headed rebel. As a young man, he had been exiled from England at the age of 18 years for disobedience to his father and was declared an outlaw by Edward the Confessor.

He returned in 1069, only to discover that the lands of his family had been confiscated by a Norman named, Ivo de Taillebuis. It is reputed that his father's and brother's heads were displayed on spikes at the front of his house.

Hereward is reputed to have killed fourteen Normans in retaliation. He conducted a rebellion against the Normans in Ely alongside aides from Denmark. They stormed Peterborough Cathedral and confiscated treasures from the Norman abbot, Turold of Fecamp in order to help secure power and wealth away from the Normans.

William the Conqueror sent an army against Hereward at Ely, but the surrounding countryside was apparently so marshy that many of William's soldiers drowned. This occurred three times. Then, Hereward disguised himself as a potter in order to enter their camp to try to find out what their future plans were to attack him.

Despite Hereward's cunning, he was betrayed by Abbot Thurston of Ely, who accepted a bribe from Williams's forces, to show them a safe path through the marshes. Morcar was captured and imprisoned but Hereward escaped into the Fens. One version of the story suggests that William I was going to pardon Hereward but died before this happened. Sadly, the Norman forces eventually found Hereward and killed him.

There are many versions of the ownership of the lands held by Hereward, but it is suggested that his daughter married Hugh de Evermue and their daughter married Richard de Rullos.

5.   Oger the Breton (1096) Bourne Aveland, Lincolnshire

Oger is said to have been the 'biggest landowner in history'. He came to England with William in the Conquest, in 1066, and was rewarded for his loyalty by gaining much land, especially around Bourne. In the Doomsday Book, there were nineteen entries for land in the Bourne area and he seemed to own all of them.

6.   William de Rollos Lord of Bourne

Rollos means 'a man of rank'. The name appears in William I's family. Having no children, he passed his inheritance to his niece, Adelina de Rollos.

7.   Adelina de Rollos

Adelina married Baldwin FitzGilbert de Clare; however, interestingly and rather unusually, he did not automatically gain her lands, but Henry I conferred these on him.

Norman Ancestors before Adeliza and Gilbert FitzRichard

A. **Richard 'The Fearless' (943-996) Count of Rouen + Emma of Paris + Gunnor.**

His father was William Longsword Sprota who was possibly William The Conqueror's grandfather. He was an educated man and was commissioned to write the, 'De Moribus et actis primorum Normanniae dueum'[1] (On the customs and deeds of the First Dukes of Normandy) under the custody of Louis IV. He is reputed as having helped to get the French crown for his brother-in-law, Hugh Capet. He also introduced feudalism or 'greatly expanded it' in Normandy.[2]

Sadly, his first wife, Emma died but later he apparently fell in love with a forester's wife, named, Seinfreda. Being a woman of virtue, she refused his advances but introduced him to her unmarried sister, Gunnor. Obviously not as virtuous as her sister, she had several children by him. However, Richard did marry her, and the children were legitimised. It is from his marriage with Gunnor that he produced his heir.

B. **Geoffrey, Count de Brionne FitzRichard Count of Eu (aka Godfre) (962-1015) + Lasceline de Turqueville**

He lived in the castle of Brionne which was situated just two miles from the coastline of Normandy thus he was in one of the first defensive positions should the English cross the Channel for an invasion.

C. **Gilbert Count of Brionne Count of Eu (1000-1040) (House of Normandy/de Clare)**

Gilbert was an influential nobleman in the Duchy of Normandy and was a guardian of William II.

He accompanied William the Conqueror in the conquest and was granted lands to become one of the most influential noble families in England. His descendants became very powerful and ruled over Ireland, Scotland and England. He was known as one of the 'Marcher Lords'.

Had Lord Brionne, 'not been murdered, the senior house of de Clare would probably have been titled 'de Brionne.'' He was murdered when riding peacefully near Eschafor.

D. Richard FitzGilbert (1035-1090) 1st Lord de Clare + Rohese Giffard (1034 -1113)

Richard came to England in the Conquest serving as joint 'Judiciar' in William's absence and managed to supress a revolt. He was styled, 'de Bienfaite' de Clare and of Tonbridge.[3] He received the lordship of Clare in Suffolk where parts of his castle are still in existence. Indeed, it is this castle that seems to be a good model for the castle in Bourne. He was considered to be the eighth richest landowner in England.

When William I died, Richard was opposed to William Rufus inheriting the throne and had joined with other barons, including Bishop Odo, William I's half- brother against him.

It would appear that he later died in a monastery.

Wikipedia suggests that Rufus did not marry or produce an heir, possibly because he was a homosexual. It continues to say that he enjoyed lust and sodomy but was a wise ruler. He was killed by an arrow through the neck but the circumstances of this occurrence are not clear.

On his death, his brother Henry I quickly took William's throne.

E. Gilbert FitzRichard de Clare de Tonbridge (1066-1117) + Adeliza de Clermont

Gilbert was born in Clare, Suffolk and was buried in Tonbridge. He continued to fortify his castle in Tonbridge and like his father, he was opposed to William Rufus. However, his castle was stormed, he was wounded and taken prisoner. His fortunes must have improved, however, as he was in attendance at the death of William Rufus. Later he attended the Christmas court of Henry I.

When Henry I succeeded in taking Cardigan Castle from the Welsh, Gilbert made a plea to him that his lands should be restored to him; he

> 'was awarded the Lordship of Cardigan and he was given the castle'.

Merger of the Bourne Family and the Normans

F./7. Baldwin FitzGilbert, Lord of Bourne, de Meulles and Sheriff of Exeter (1092-1194) + Adeline de Rollos

Baldwin was actually his father's third son but his eldest brother, Richard, was slain when their lands were, 'harried' by Morgan ap Owen after Henry I's death.[4]

King Stephen gave him money to hire troops but Baldwin failed to strike a single blow in the 'Battle of Lincoln'. However, when King Stephen tried to address his troops, his voice was so weak that Baldwin had to address them for him.

He fought bravely but both he and the King were taken prisoner and Stephen was deposed from the throne. Matilda ruled for a short time following this 'Angevine' victory but the throne soon went to her son, Henry II.

Baldwin had married the niece of William de Rollos, Adelina and so the title of Lord of Bourne should naturally have passed to him as her husband but for some reason, the title and properties had to be granted by Henry I.

Baldwin is credited with building the Norman Castle on the Well Head in Bourne, possibly between 1123-1139 and also the Abbey Church of St. Peter and St. Paul in 1186. It is

reported that his castle was a motte and bailey castle built on a concentric plan, the motte being a castle with an artificial mound, in order to hold a defensible structure or keep.

Baldwin is buried in the churchyard in Bourne, next to the church, but I have yet to locate his grave.

8. Emma FitzGilbert de Clare (1114-1168) + Hugh Wac Ne'grevillea (1114)

Emma was born in Bourne 'Abbey,' probably meaning in the castle and was buried in Thorney. She was the heiress of Bourne and inherited Bourne lands despite having an older brother.

The story goes that her brother was imprisoned in Lincoln and in order to secure his release, she had to marry a knight who served the lords of Lincoln. The knight chosen was Hugh le Wac, son of Geoffrey le Wac and so the name Clare became less important and the eventual spelling of Wac became Wake.

9. Baldwin Wake I (1137-1198) + Agnes du Honnet

Baldwin became the King's Constable in England. He also now owned Hereward's lands in Witham, Barholm, the Deepings and the Fens.

He was a feudal Lord of Bourne and also a benefactor.

10. Baldwin le Wac II (1184-1224) + Isabel de Briwere (1184-1224)

Baldwin was born in Bilsworth/Bisworth/Blisworth, Northants and his wife was born in Stoke, Devonshire.

He had been imprisoned by King John in 1207 but his pardon came in 1210 when he was regranted his lands in both England and Guernsey.

He was killed on 20th July by a crossbow arrow in the siege of Gascony.

11. Hugh Wake I of Liddell, Lord of Bourne (1202-1241) + Joan Stuteville (1219)

He was born in Bilsworth but died on a crusade in Jerusalem, accompanying Simon de Montfort, on 18th December 1241, in the reign of Henry III.

His titles included that of Sheriff of Yorkshire and Constable of Scarborough Castle.

He had been in disgrace earlier for marrying Joan without a royal licence in 1229, however, it seems Henry granted him a pardon.

12. Baldwin Wake III Lord of Bourne (1236-1282) + Howise de Quincey

Baldwin was also born in Blisworth and died in Liddell, Cumberland.

13. John Wake 1st Baron of Liddell (1268-1300) + Joan FitzBernard Lady Joan Wake

John was born in Blisworth, Northants.

In 1298, he fought at the 'Battle of Falkirk' and became known as a warrior of repute also assisting Edward Bruce to invade Scotland. However, he fell foul of the King and was imprisoned; later he was restored to his lands.

Edward III made him the Governor of the Channel Isles.

He was involved in a plot with his brother-in-law, Edmund of Woodstock, Earl of Kent, the youngest son of Edward III, against Isabella and Mortimer but he suffered defeat and was killed.

14. Thomas Wake 2nd Baron Wake of Liddell (1297-1349) + Blanche Lady Wake (1305- 1380)

Thomas was a councillor to the young Edward III and was a favourite with Edward II, opposing Isabella and Mortimer. He was summoned to Parliament in 1295, being involved in a plot with his brother-in-law, Edmund Woodstock.

In 1328, he had to surrender following an unsuccessful rising against Isabella and Mortimer; he was fined and deprived of his offices.

In 1330, Edward III spent a week at Bourne Castle, obviously a guest of Blanche as Thomas may still have been in disgrace.

In 1331, his offices were restored to him when Mortimer died and he was then awarded the Governorship of the Chanel Isles. In 1340, disaster happened again, as Edward III imprisoned him. He was still a man of power but it seems that his time spent in Bourne would have been limited.

His wife, Blanche, eldest daughter of Henry III, Lord of Lancaster, was apparently a very strong-willed woman. After the death of Thomas, she had a complaint lodged against her and her council in Bourne, by a Dominican friar, John Lyte, in 1358.

She had allegedly done him and his church many wrongs in Ely. However, the Bishop of Ely had burned down some of her houses and probably she was seeking revenge.

The Pope issued some very gruesome instructions to the bishop in Lincoln saying he should, "curse all that did wrong; and those who are dead, and guilty in this matter, should be dug out of their graves, and cast out of sanctuary".[5] (Not a very loving and forgiving Pope in those days!)

When the bishop came to Bourne to carry out this sentence, Lady Blanche was ready for him and "much manslaughter was caused by this matter for those that bought the command were for the most part killed"[6]

Blanche emerged the victor and the lineage of the castle was undisturbed.

Thomas and Blanche died childless and consequently the inheritance of the castle and lands went to his sister, John Wake's daughter, Margaret.

15. Margaret 3rd Baroness Wake of Liddell (1305-1380) + Edmund Earl of Woodstock Plantagenet (1301-1376)

Dates may be adrift here…Wikipedia says her dates are 1297-1349.

Her husband, Edmund, was the sixth son of Edward I and younger half-brother of Edward II (interestingly, her first husband, John Comyn was murdered by Robert the Bruce at the 'Battle of Bannockburn') but sadly their only child died as a toddler.

She was obviously not a lucky lady as Edmund was executed for treason in 1330 and her two sons by him, both having been the Earls of Kent, died. Margaret, whilst pregnant, was confined to Salisbury Castle and her brother, Thomas Wake I, Baron Wake was also accused of treason but later pardoned.

Her luck then changed as Edward III, on reaching his majority, was able to overthrow the regents and took Margaret and her children into his care and 'treated them as his own family'[7]. Margaret succeeded as, Baroness Wake of Liddell but died of the plague.

Altogether Margaret had ten children but perhaps the most famous and most interesting was Joan, 'The Fair Maid of Kent'.

16. Joan Countess of Kent (1328- 1385) + Thomas Holland + William Montagu + Edward Woodstock (Black Prince)

Now here was a lady who did not live a reticent life!

Joan was born in Oxfordshire and inherited the lands of Bourne when Blanche died, although there is little evidence to suggest that she spent much time here.

She was renowned for her beauty which obviously made her an attractive woman to the men in the court.

Her main claim for fame is that when Edward III was looking for a title for a new heraldic honour, following his victory at Crecy in 1346. Joan's garter fell to the floor whilst attending a glittering ball in Paris. Edward had to think no further; he fastened her garter around his knee uttering the immortal words, 'Honi soit qui mal y pense'.

The honour became known as the 'Order of the Garter' in which there would only ever be 24 members of the highest nobility. Many of her descendants were awarded the title, including Margaret Beaufort.

Joan obviously fell in love at the very precocious age of twelve and married her beau, Thomas Holland I, Earl of Kent, in secret, a marriage known as 'per verba de praesenti'[8] but perfectly legal and witnessed.

However, Thomas was almost immediately sent to France to fight in the 100 Year War. Whether or not Joan kept her secret, or simply wondered if Thomas might not return from war or whether there was pressure from her parents to marry well, within the year, Joan married again, this time to William Montagu.

Had Thomas not returned from the wars there would have been no problem, but he did return, and Joan obviously preferred him to William.

William imprisoned Joan to keep her to himself but Thomas raised money to get a dispensation from the Pope, who was in Avignon, and eighteen months later succeeded in getting her marriage to William annulled.

Thomas went on to become the Earl of Salisbury, being recognised as both a soldier and diplomat. He died of an illness in Normandy and was buried in Stamford, Lincs. In her will, Joan stated that she would wish to be buried next to him. Together, he and Joan had three children.

Joan went on to marry her third husband, Edward, 'the Black Prince', grandson of Edward I.

In this marriage she gave birth to the King of England, Richard II and became known as the Princess of Aquitaine and Gascony. On Edward's death she was known as 'The Mother of the King'.

Joan, who also had the titles of 4th Countess of Kent and 5th Baroness Wake of Liddell, lived in Wallingford Castle in her later years and died on 25th July 1445, in Dunbar Castle. She was buried at Greyfriars, Stamford, Lincs.

17. **Thomas Holland II 1st Earl of Kent 1st Duke of Surrey Baron Holland 1st Duke of Exeter (1350-1397) + Alice FitzAlan (1350-1416)**

Thomas was also a soldier and a captain of the English Forces in Aquitaine, fighting under his stepfather, 'The Black Prince'. He was a counsellor to Edward III.

In 1374, he became a 'Knight of the Garter' and in 1381, became the Earl of Kent.

When Thomas died, his funeral took place in Westminster Abbey, but he was buried in Bourne. Again, I have a yet to discover his grave in Bourne Abbey's graveyard.

(Thomas Holland III Duke of Kent (1372-1400) + Joan Stafford)

Thomas died childless. It appears that in 1400, Thomas was beheaded by a mob of angry citizens because of his role in the Easter Risings. He was in opposition to Henry IV, who had captured Thomas's relation, Richard II, allegedly starving him to death in prison, so taking the throne from him.

18. Margaret Holland de Beaufort (1385-1439) + John Beaufort 1st Earl of Somerset (1385 - 1410)

Margaret was born in Bermondsey and was buried in Canterbury Cathedral. Her father was Thomas Holland, 2nd Earl of Kent and the son of Joan, 'The Fair Maid of Kent'.

She was a noted English noble woman and was also invested as a 'Lady Companion of the Order of the Garter'.

John Beaufort I, her husband, was the first of the four illegitimate children on John of Gaunt. The children were legitimised by Richard II, once John had married his mistress, Katherine Swynford. The portcullis symbol was adopted by the family and the name 'Beaufort' was adopted from their castle in France.

He became the Admiral of the Irish Fleet, Constable of Dover Castle and Warden of the Cinque Ports. He helped Richard II against the 'Lords Appellant' and was further rewarded by becoming Lord Somerset and Marquess of Aquitaine.

He continued to support Richard II throughout the time when Henry IV was banished from England in 1398. However, when Henry returned victorious, he confiscated all of John's titles, with the exception of Earl of Somerset.

Beaufort died in 1410, in the Tower of London. Margaret Holland de Beaufort, his widow, married his nephew Thomas of Lancaster, Duke of Clarence but they did not have any children. She died at St Saviour's Abbey, Bermondsey, in London and is interred in the middle of both of her husbands in a carved alabaster tomb.

Although The Wars of the Roses are credited to the warring families of Edward III, Margaret also seemed to play a part in the wars through the children she produced with John Beaufort and how they contributed to the warring factions.

One daughter, Joan, married James I Scotland; John Beaufort II, 1st Duke Somerset, married Margaret Beauchamp, the mother of Margaret Beaufort, (Lancaster); Eleanor Holland married Edmund Mortimer and their daughter, Anne Mortimer, was the mother of Richard Duke of York, firmly on the opposite side to the future Margaret Beaufort.

19. **John Beaufort II (1404-1444) + Margaret Beauchamp (1410-1482)**

Parents of Margaret Beaufort (details written previously).

20. **Margaret Beaufort, Countess of Richmond (1443-1509) + John de la Pole (1442-1492) + Edmund Tudor (1430-1456) + Henry Stafford Duke of Buckingham (1455-1483) + Thomas Stanley (1435-1456)**

21. **Henry VII**

22. **Henry VIII**

23. **Henry Fitzroy** (illegitimate son with Bessie Blount)

24. **Sir William Daborne Heckington de Bourne (1450-1587) + Alice Walcot (1454)**

I have checked William's age of death in several places and it seems that he may have lived until he was 115 years old! Bourne is supposed to be a healthy place for sleeping and also for living to a ripe old age. Indeed, my own father's family, who were all dwellers of Bourne, lived into their 90's, so maybe he was a 'long liver'!

Both he and Alice were born in Bourne and the castle came into his possession; he may have bought the land as it seemed to have sunken into decay after the Cromwellian soldiers had used the possible ruins of the castle and lands as an encampment, leaving in about 1645.

25. Lady Jane Heckington (1500-1588) + Richard Cecil (1495-1553)

Jane was a very pious lady and married Richard Cecil, a nobleman, politician, courtier and Master of Burghley in the parish of Stamford. He rose to favour in the court of Henry VIII and became the High Sheriff of Northamptonshire.

He was present at the 'Field of Cloth of Gold' 1520, when Henry VIII met Francis I of France for a royal summit meeting, both with the intention of outshining each other in both prowess and wealth.

Apparently, Richard Cecil gained much of his fortune from the plunder of the monasteries. He is buried at St Margaret's, Westminster.

26. William Cecil 1st Baron Burghley KG. PC Lord High Treasurer (1520-1598) + Mary Cheke

Here is another famous and influential person who was born here in Bourne. He was born in the manor, which became known as 'The Bull Hotel' but later became the 'Burghley Arms'. A plaque can be seen on the wall outside to acknowledge this as his birthplace.

William was the chief advisor to Elizabeth I at the onset of her reign. In many ways, Elizabeth was so young, that he was almost recognised in a kingly position. He had an incredible network of spies working for him and would have saved England from many threats to the throne.

William married Mary Cheke but she had no position or wealth of her own and Richard Cecil his father, banned the marriage. William therefore married her secretly.

She proved her worth to him and as William was frequently away on court business, Mary was largely responsible for overseeing the great house's construction in Stamford.

Today, this is the venue of 'The Burghley Horse Trials' and is frequented by many of our present royal family. Indeed, Princess Anne and her daughter Zara, have been riders here, on courses designed by Captain Mark Phillips.

Sadly, in William's efforts to save the crown from the threat of Mary Queen of Scots and a threatened take over by Scotland, he managed to get Elizabeth to authorise the beheading of Mary. This saved her throne, but he fell from her favour as Elizabeth did not want this death on her conscience.

He is recognised in history as a great statesman and politician.

He is buried in St Martin's Church, Stamford, Lincs. situated near the great estate of Burghley House.

27. Robert Cecil 1st Earl of Salisbury KG, PC Baron Cecil of Essendon, Viscount Cranborne (1563 -1612) + Elizabeth Brooke

William's son, Robert is apparently quite a controversial character in history but was also a brilliant politician. He was the person who not only instigated the union of Scotland and England by appointing James VI of Scotland to be James I of England but he also was the one to uncover the Gunpowder Plot of 1605.

It has been suggested that he might have been involved in the plotting but like his father, he had a very good spy network and this involvement could well have been a ploy to discover their plans covertly and then thwart them.

One story I love, written by Philippa Gregory, is 'Earthly Joys', which reveals much about Robert. Interestingly, he had a gardener called, John Tradescant, who travelled the world in order to bring back a huge variety of plants. He was given six conkers and was so charmed by them that he nurtured them carefully and they soon began to flourish. I very much enjoy the fact that the Cecil family are therefore, through their gardener, responsible for all our horse chestnut trees today.

The lands of Bourne Castle, or the Well Head, then passed from the Cecil family to be owned by Bourne United Charities. They have improved this area with a playground for children and made a beautiful avenue of trees leading from South Street, which looks stunning when in blossom in April.

The field abutting South Street has been converted into 'The Garden of Remembrance' with its own cenotaph. It is all worth a visit for the historian or for anyone wishing for a tranquil walk.

Should you wish to research any of these characters, there is far more information available, but I wanted to give a simple picture of Margaret's amazing ancestors especially as they have been the owners of Bourne Castle.

Never did I imagine, as a child, that my playground had once been owned by the famous/infamous Henry VIII!

The dates found here can be questioned. It depends on which historical information is accessed but they are 'approximately accurate'.

10

'The Castelle of Brunne'

Peak's Account from J. D. Birkbeck's book
'A History of Bourne'

According to J. D. Birkbeck's book, now sadly out of print, Peak's account 1809 states the following:

'The castelle of Brunne ys a verrye ancient portliecastelle, seytewate neare Peterspoole. It contaynes thre principal wardes; on the north side ys the porter's lodgewch ys now reuinoose and in decaye by reason ye floors of ye upper house ys decayed and very necessarie to be repayred.

"The dungeon ye sett of a little moate, made with mens hands for the most parte as it were square.

It ys a fare and prattie building with IV square toures rounde about ye same dungeon. Upon ye roofe of ye said toures ye tryme walkes and a fare prospect of ye Fenes, and ye said dungeonys ye halle, chambres and all other manner of houses and offices for ye lorde and his traine.

"The south syde therof servethe for ye lords and ladys lodgings and underneigh them ys ye prisone, and ye wyne cellar (hooray!) with ye schollorie.

"Over ye moate yt surrounds ye castelle is a fare drawe bridge, ye moate ys verie fresh and deepe, there ys also a fare parke belonging ye castelle."[67]

Birkbeck goes on to say that a John Leyland, who made an antiquarian tour through England between 1534 and 1543, mentions that 'unlike Peak, he found the castle very greatly ruined, with little earthwork remaining. "there appeare grete diches, and the dungeon hil of an auncient castel agayne the west side of the priorie, sumwhat distant from it on the other side of the striate backwarde: it longidd to the Lorde Wake, and much service of the Wake fe is done to this castelle ; and every feodarie knowith his station and his place of service".

A later reference to the castle is in an entry in the parish registers during the Civil War period. It says, "11th October 1645, the garrison of Bourne Castle began". Birkbeck makes the comment that the Castle must have been in better repair than Leyland suggested or, he suggests, that perhaps the garrison of Cromwell's soldiers merely made their encampment there.

Further to his studies he suggests that 'an outer bailey or courtyard covered an area of about eight acres and was bounded by St. Peter's Pool and the Bourne Eau, right round from the Pool to what is now South Street; thus a second, or outer moat was created. The keep was therefore protected, on the south by a

---

[67] J. D. Birkbeck (pp*)

single moat running close beside it and on the other three sides by two moats, one fairly close in and the other at some distance away, the latter being in fact the river itself.'[68]

---

[68] "Peak's M S account..."is mentioned in W Marrat Op. cit. and in J. Moore: "Account of the Hundred of Aveland", 1809 (L.A.O. Monson 7/40/6.

11

Collyweston

Before the Covid 19 lockdown in March 2020, we ventured to Collyweston to find any traces of the magnificent palace that had been one of Margaret's favourite residences.

On enquiry in the village, few people could offer much information at first and few were aware that a castle had ever existed. Finally, we were pointed in the right direction.

From Bourne, on reaching the crossroads, it is necessary to turn right, past the church and the village shop and to continue down the hill. At the bottom, one must follow the road to the right and at the end of that road are the signs of the existence of the castle.

There on the left-hand side is a gate with a sign saying 'Palace Gardens', with the following information:

'Following Henry's success at Bosworth and in recognition of his mother's dedication, Henry awarded her the manor of Collyweston in the great grant of 1487'.

It was at this time that he granted Margaret the 'Femme sole' giving her the right to manage this property and improve it in any way she saw fit.

On entering the gate of the garden, apart from being adorned by a multitude of mole hills (the mole catcher arrived as we left), it was possible to see the remains of the walls that surrounded this garden.

The most convincing and striking feature, however, was the imposing sundial in stonework. Certainly, this would have graced any royal residence and it would seem logical that this was about the only real evidence of its past owner. Margaret took a great delight in her garden and planned it very carefully with her gardener, William Love. She apparently had orchards, a herb garden and a deer park.

Sadly, there is no further evidence of her home here. Several properties have been built on the land that would once have been a part of the castle but there is evidence that some of these, as in Bourne, could have used the stones from the castle for the 'new' constructions.

However, we were delighted to find that in the church there is a display dedicated to Margaret that reveals much of her history.

The church has an unusual outbuilding attached to it on the right-hand side at the front. It was here where Margaret would have been sitting during the church services so that she could be apart from the rest of the worshippers but still hear the mass.

Apparently, this chapel contained many beautiful objects including decorative altar cloths; one was decorated with her symbol of marguerites and another was made of red velvet which was later given to Christ's College. Also, there were gold cups, salt cellars, and 'plate featuring saints including St Anthony, St George,

St Anne and St Margaret.'[69] The holy water was in a container made from gold.

There is a small window, now bricked in, but on the church wall side and quite high up where Margaret must have sat to hear the Church Service. There must have been some steps to reach the window but they are no longer in existence.

It is in here, in this room, where the small museum can be found which displays pictures of her and includes a copy of her signature, 'Margaret R.' The museum has been established by Chris Close at 'Chaps'. There is an ongoing excavation being conducted by the local history group of 'Chaps' and maybe in the future, a ground map of the palace will be available.

All we know at present, is that the site had been excavated in the past but then built over and that all that remains are fishponds, terraces and a tythe barn, now converted into a house.

It is agreed that there was once a dungeon, a jewel house, a courthouse, chapel, library, counting house and a great parlour. The main room was called the 'Queen's Chamber' and according to www.englishmonarchs.co.uk, Margaret, 'ensured the house was furnished as befitted her wealth and rank'. Indeed, she had many important visitors to her palace. When her granddaughter went to Scotland to marry James IV of Scotland, it was from here that she began her journey north.

The castle in Collyweston was about three miles south of Stamford, Lincolnshire and was built by Sir William Porter in the early fifteenth century. In 1441 Ralph, Lord Cromwell enlarged it and on his death in 1455, it became the property of 'Warwick the Kingmaker' but soon passed to George, the Duke of Clarence. This,

---

[69] N. Tallis (pp*)

no doubt, was part of the political agreement and reward when George joined Warwick in opposition to Edward IV.

After George's execution at the hand of his brother, it became a Crown property, eventually falling into the hands of Henry VII following his victory at the Battle of Bosworth and then gifted by him to his mother.

Margaret, being wealthy and 'femme sole', set about making Collyweston a palace fit for a queen. Little is mentioned about the exterior of the palace other than there were two clock houses, but the interior was particularly lavish.

Most of her possessions were decorated with her family symbols, even her carving knives were adorned with the portcullis. She indulged in rich fabrics and other luxuries and even had running water throughout the palace.

She had between two and four hundred servants which suggests the palace must have been of some significant size. One servant, Henry Parker, remained with her for forty years; he seemed to admire her greatly and she had a fondness for him.

Despite her wealth and independence, she must have been a fair and just person to have commanded such loyalty. Certainly, she looked after the educational needs of the children within her household and many nobles asked her to be a 'ward' for their children.

It was here that Margaret had her administrative centre and was very active in running the community and the administration of justice in the King's name.

Appendices

Appendix 1

Succession of the Royal Family

(Margaret Beaufort is the one link from William the Conqueror to our present Royal Family!)

1066	William I The Conqueror
1087	William II
1100	Henry I
1135	Stephen
1154	Henry II
1189	Richard I
1199	John
1216	Henry III
1272	Edward I
1307	Edward II
1327	Edward III
1377	Richard II
1399	Henry IV

1413   Henry V + Katherine de Valois + Owen Tudor

1422   Henry VI Edmund Tudor + Margaret Beaufort
1461   Edward IV

1483   Edward V

1483   Richard III

                                    1485   Henry VII

                                    1509   Henry VIII

James IV Scotland +   1547   Edward VI

Margaret (Margaret   1553   Mary I

Beaufort's granddaughter)   1558   Elizabeth I

James V Scotland

Mary Queen of Scots

James VI Scotland   A.K.A.

                                    1603   James I

                                    1625   Charles I

                                    1660   Charles II

                                    1685   James II

                                    1689   Mary II +
                                                  William III

                                    1702   Anne (also daughter

                                                    of James II)

1603 James 1

Elizabeth (granddaughter)
+ Frederick V King of Bohemia

Sophia (daughter) + Ernest Agustus

Elector of Hanover)

1714	George I
1727	George II
1760	George III
1820	George IV
1830	William IV
1837	Victoria (niece of George IV)
1901	Edward VII
1910	George V
1936	Edward VIII
1936	George VI
1952	Elizabeth II

Appendix 2

The Family of Edward III

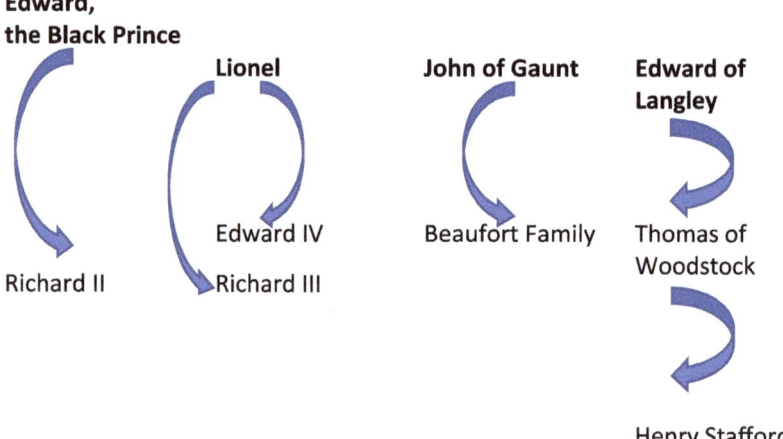

**Edward,
the Black Prince**

Lionel

John of Gaunt

**Edward of
Langley**

Edward IV

Beaufort Family

Thomas of
Woodstock

Richard II

Richard III

Henry Stafford

Appendix 3

**Margaret's Family Line
(Main Line of Decent)**

Richard the Fearless + Emma (943 – 996)	Leofric + Godiva
Geoffrey de Brionne (Count of Eu) + Aubree	(Hereward (1035-1072))
Gilbert + Adeliza of Flanders (1040)	Aelfgar (Earl of Mercia)
Richard FitzGilbert + Adeliza de Clermont (1117)	Lord Morcar (1067)
	Oger the Breton (1086)
	William De Rollos. (Lord of Bourne)
Baldwin FitzGilbert de Clare + Adelina De Rollos (1154)	Adelina (1130) Niece

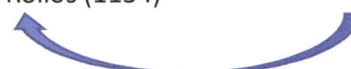

Hugh Wac Lord of the Manor (1144) + Emma De Clare

Baldwin Wac/Wake I (1137-1198)

Baldwin Wac/Wake II (1184-1224)

Hugh Wake (1212-1241)

Baldwin Wake III (1236-1282)

John Wake Ist Baron Wake of Liddell (1268-1300)

Thomas Wake + Blanche (1297-1349)

Thomas Wake's sister Margaret Wake + John Comyn (1305-1380)

Thomas Holland I (1314 – 1360) + Joan Wake + Black Prince (1328 – 1385)

Thomas Holland II   Richard II

Margaret Holland (sister of Edmund Holland) + John Beaufort I (1373-1410)

John Beaufort II (1404-1444) + Margaret Beauchamp (1410-1482)

Margaret Beaufort (1443-1509)

Appendix Four

Beaufort Family Lineage

William the Conqueror (Duke of Normandy) 1066 + Matilda of Flanders

William II (William Rufus – son of William the Conqueror) 1087

Henry I (Duke of Normandy - son of William the Conqueror) 1100

Stephen de Blois (1135) (Duke of Normandy)

Matilda + Geoffrey Plantagenet (Count d'Anjou)

Henry II (1154)

Richard I 1189   John (Brother) (1199)

Henry III (1216)

Edward I (1272)

Edward II (1307)

Edward III (1327)

John of Gaunt + Katherine Swynford

John Beaufort I + Margaret Holland

John Beaufort II + Margaret Beauchamp

Margaret Beaufort

Appendix Five

Margaret Beaufort's Descendancy from Edward III

Edward III (Plantagenet)

Henry IV

Henry V + Katherine De Valois + Owen Tudor

Henry VI + Margaret d'Anjou

Edmund Tudor + Margaret Beaufort

Henry VII (Tudor)

Henry VIII (sister Margaret + James IV of Scotland)

Edward VI

Mary Tudor

Elizabeth I

James I (VI of Scotland) (Stuarts)

Index

Bibliography

The Life of Henry VII (written 1500 – 1502) Bernard Andre in the translation by Daniel Hobbins (2016)

A History of Bourne   J. D. Birkbeck (1976)

'Mornynge Remembrance'   John Fisher

Through Early English Books online (2020)

'Non Time History'   Steven Giullari (2020)

The Red Queen   Philippa Gregory (2010)

Earthly Joys   Philippa Gregory (1998)

The Portcullis   House of Commons Information Office

Bourne and its Castle   Kenneth Jacobs (2010)

The Wars of the Roses   Matthew Lewis (Aug. 2016)

Margaret Beaufort: Mother of the Tudor Dynasty

                                                      Elizabeth Norton (2010)

Winter King: The Dawn of Tudor England

                                                      Thomas Penn (Sept. 2011)

Richard III   W. Shakespeare (1593)

Romeo and Juliet   W. Shakespeare (1595 -97)

Uncrowned Queen: The Fateful Life of Margaret Beaufort Tudor Matriarch — Nicola Tallis (Oct. 2019)

'Polydore Angelica Historia' — Vergil, quoted in N. Tallis (2019)

Kings & Queens of Britain — David Williamson (1991)

Prisoners of the Tower — Sebastian Edwards for Historic Royal Palaces (2004)

'Bourne and its Abbey and Castle' — E. Venables in Associated Architectural Society (*)

Henry VII — Neville Williams (1973)

Chambers Cyclopedia of English Literature — Tallis

'De Occupationne Regni Angeli per Riccardum Tercium' — D. Mancini trans. and ed. as C A J Armstrong in 'The Usurpation of Richard III (2nd edition, Oxford 1969)

www.ancestory.com

www.englishmonarchs.co.uk

www.books.google.co.uk

www.wikipedia.com

References

Chapter Nine

Owners of the Castle

1. Leofric Wikipediand Godiva Wikipedia

2. Aelfgar Wikidedia

3. Morcar Wikidedia

4. Hereward the Wake Birkbeck J D A History of Bourne Charles Kingsley www. Britannica.com Goodreads Wikipedia

5. Ogar https://opendomesday.org

6. William Rollos

7. Adelina de Rollos Legacy Family Tree Program from Melennia Corporation and Adobe Dreamweaver

A. Richard the Fearless Encyclopedia Britannia cc by licence

B. Geoffrey de Brionne Wikipedia (Wilson and Currator)

C. Gilbert de Brionne Wikipedia

D. Richard FitzGilbert Wikipedia

E. Gilbert FitzRichard Wikipedia

F. Baldwin FitzGilbert Wikipedia

8. Emma FitzGilbert The Peerage ancestors.family search.org Geni.com

9. Baldwin Wake Geni.com managed by Bernard Assof

10. Lord Baldwin II Geni.com

11. Hugh Wake of Liddell Geni Burk's Peerage

12. Baldwin Wake III Geni.com

13. John Wake Wikipedia

14. Thomas Wake Baron Wake of Liddell Birkbeck J D

15. Margaret 3rd Baroness Wake of Liddell Wikipedia

16. Joan Countess of Kent Wikipedia.org www.englishmonarchs. co.uk Anne O'Brian 'The Shadow Queen' Birkbeck J D

17. Thomas Holland III Birkbeck J D

18. Margaret Holland de Beaufort Wikipedia

19. John Beaufort II Wikipedia

20. Margaret Beaufort Countess of Richmond

21. Henry VII see other notes

22. Henry VIII see other notes

23. Hernry FitzRoy Google

24. William Heckington Ancestry.com

25. Lady Jane Heckington Ancestry.com

26. William Cecil Wikipedia

27. Robert Cecil Wikipedia, Philippa Gregory

Acknowledgements

In writing this history of Margaret Beaufort and her links to my hometown of Bourne, I must acknowledge the help and support received from all of my family and friends, especially my husband Ken; I could not have completed this without it!

A special thanks must go to my son for the design of the book cover and to my daughter Liz Salmon for providing wine and her invaluable I.T. support.

Indebted thanks must also go to Sue Slowey, my proof reader and past English teacher-who better!

I would like to thank Steve Giullari for his encouragement and knowledge of the castle and also for his advice and help given so unstintingly. Also to Jonathan Smith for his interest and encouragement and Brenda and Jim Jones for their work in sustaining the Bourne Heritage Centre.

Thank you all!

The Author

Margaret has always had a deep love of her hometown of Bourne. Indeed, she can trace her paternal ancestry back to the 1660s in the Bourne Abbey registers.

She attended the Bourne Abbey Primary School and was later educated at Bourne Grammar School; it was here that her interest in history began, with her history teachers, J. D. Birkbeck and his wife, Margaret.

Although Margaret has always enjoyed history, even teaching this subject for a while, she would not count herself as a historian. She has always enjoyed sport and trained in this subject at 'Carnegie College' in Leeds. However, she taught English for most of her career at firstly 'Bourne Grammar School' and later at Bourne's 'Robert Manning School', now known as 'Bourne Academy'. She is from a teaching family and many 'Brunnians' were taught by her well-loved mother, Mrs Audrey Scotney, at the Abbey Road School.

Margaret's husband, Ken, also a teacher at the 'Robert Manning School', is keen to preserve the heritage of Bourne and is in the latter stages of constructing a model railway of Bourne Station that will soon be ready for exhibition.

Both would admit that their main hobby now is singing, being members and soloists in 'Stamford Gilbert and Sullivan Players' and the 'Stamford Singers Concert Party'. They are members of the 'Bourne Abbey Choir' and perform in their own entertainment group, 'Tinderbox', along with Dee Hill, Laurence Lewis and their accompanist, Liz Hill. Both Margaret and Ken also enjoy solo roles in their local pantomime group, 'Tomorrow's Dream'.

However, having become fascinated with the life and achievements of Margaret Beaufort, Margaret sees her as one of the most influential women in history. Consequently, she was puzzled as to why little to no mention has ever been made to link Margaret Beaufort to our local area and in particular Bourne.

She hopes that this book will help to rectify this oversight and give the mother of the Tudor dynasty the recognition that she deserves.

Margaret Wainwright standing in front of Margaret Beaufort's heraldic symbols St John's College Cambridge.

(Note the additions of the surmounting crowns added after she became the 'King's Mother'.)

The **TUDOR** Dynasty

Margaret Beaufort

of

Bourne,

Collyweston, Maxey and Deeping

Margaret Wainwright

Lightning Source UK Ltd.
Milton Keynes UK
UKHW020335181220
375433UK00001B/21